By the same author

The Golden String
Return to the Center
The Marriage of East & West
The Cosmic Revelation

Christ in India

Essays towards a Hindu-Christian Dialogue

BEDE GRIFFITHS

 Templegate Publishers, Springfield, Illinois

To Shata Gopa and Mahalaksmi
in token of Hindu-Christian friendship

Contents

CONTENTS

A New Introduction

THE ESSAYS in this book were all written between the years 1955 and 1965, when I first came to India. They mark therefore an important stage not only in my life but also in that of the Church and the western world. It was the time of the Vatican Council when the Catholic Church for the first time began to open itself to the religions of the East and when the cult of Eastern religions, particularly of Zen Buddhism, began to spread widely in the West. These essays record the stages of my own discovery of Hinduism and my attempts to relate it to Christian monasticism and the theology of the Catholic Church. It was also the time when I was living as a monk of the Syrian Church in Kerala and was seeking to find the place of the Eastern Christian tradition in the life of the Church.

When I first came to India I came as a Christian and naturally saw Hinduism in the context of the theology of the Church at that time. I felt that the Eastern Churches, especially the Syrian Church, which has had such a long history in Kerala, might provide a kind of bridge between the Western Church and Indian culture. But I have come to realise that though the Syrian Church is rooted in Kerala and has in these last years recovered much of its ancient tradition, it still remains culturally a religion of the Middle East and is very far from the cultural tradition of India and the Far East. I have come therefore to see that the Indian Church, in the words of the founder of our ashram, Jules Monchanin, has to be neither Latin or Greek or Syrian, but 'totally Indian and totally Christian.'

My aim throughout has been to find how the Indian Church, while remaining 'totally Christian', that is, totally true to the authentic tradition of Christian faith, can also be totally open to the authentic values of Hinduism. This is no easy task and many will no doubt feel that I remain too Christocentric and do not allow sufficiently for the radical transformation which the encounter with Hinduism may demand of the Church. But Hindu-Christian dialogue is only just beginning and has still a long way to go. One can only record the stages on the way as one tries to be more and more open to the truth in each tradition and to see the meeting of the two religions not only from the Christian but also from the Hindu point of view.

The other essays in the book are concerned with the social and economic condition of India. No one who has lived long in India can fail to be aware of the tremendous problem of poverty in India which, in spite of all the efforts which have been made since independence, has increased rather than diminished, in the sense that the poor have grown poorer while the rich have grown richer. In regard to this I remain a convinced disciple of Mahatma Gandhi. A great many Christians in India are convinced that a social revolution based on a Marxist analysis of society is the only answer to the needs of India. With this I entirely disagree. To me the fatal defect of Marxism and all forms of socialism is that they take for granted the present industrial system and seek to change the ownership of the means of production of wealth and the method of its distribution but not the actual system of production. But I believe with Gandhi that it is the present system of technology based on a mechanistic system of science, which is the root cause of imbalance in the world to-day.

In recent years there has been a revolution in western science as indicated by Fritjof Capra's book *The Tao of Physics* and his more recent book *The Turning Point*. In these books he shows that western science is moving from a mechanistic model of the universe from which modern technology is derived, to an organic model, a model in which human existence is seen to be an organic part in the evolution of the universe, so that nature is not dead matter to be exploited by man, as has been done in the present system, but a living organism for which man is responsible. What is sought to-day therefore is a new form of technology, which will not seek to dominate and manipulate nature but will work in harmony with nature and out of reverence for life. It was this form of technology which Schumacher envisaged in his book *Small is Beautiful* and which he sought to embody in what he called intermediate or appropriate technology.

It is this kind of technology which alone is meaningful in India and the third world and which corresponds with Gandhi's ideal of building up from the villages in which the vast majority of the people of Asia still live. It is true that the Gandhian method has failed in India so far. That is because it cannot compete with the present industrial system. But when this system begins to break down, as it will surely do, it will then be found that the Gandhian method is the only answer to the world's problems. This extends not only to the problems of economics but also to social and political problems. I firmly believe that the peace of the world will never be found as long as the present system prevails. It is only when we have learned reverence for nature that we will learn to be at peace with one another and bring peace to the world.

Bede Griffiths, Shantivanam, 1984

Introduction

MY FIRST experience of India was when I was a small boy
in the First World War. There was a convalescent camp for
soldiers in the village where I was living and one year it
was occupied by Indian soldiers. I used to go and visit the
soldiers and one of them, a Sikh, became a great friend. He
used to call me his 'little brother', and when one of the
soldiers offered me a cigarette (though I was much too
young to smoke) he would point at me and say: 'Sikh – no
smoke' (the Sikhs as a rule neither drink nor smoke). I
think that I must have felt even then a kinship with India
and for a long time, when I was at school, it was my ambition
to join the Indian Civil Service. Later, when under the influence of Tolstoy I became very strongly pacifist, I was
attracted to Mahatma Gandhi. I remember reading a life of
Lenin and Gandhi at this time and feeling how Lenin with
his belief in violence, materialism and mass organization
stood for everything which I disliked, while Gandhi with
his faith in non-violence and truth (*ahimsa* and *satya*), the
spinning-wheel and the village community, stood for all that
I admired.

I had an opportunity of meeting Gandhi after this, and
it is a lasting regret that I missed it. It was in 1931 when he
came to London to the Round Table conference and I was
staying in Bethnal Green not far from where he was. I was
undergoing a deep spiritual crisis at the time, which led to
my becoming a monk soon after, and this prevented me from
seeing him, but he and his conception of life remained fixed
in my mind as an ideal which never left me. At the same

time I became aware of the spiritual principles which under-
lay Gandhi's way of life by reading the Dhammapada and
the Bhagavad Gita.* This was my first introduction to Indian
spirituality and it left an indelible impression on my mind.
The sense of an ultimate reality beyond this world of space
and time, whether it was called Brahman or Atman or
Nirvana, which alone gave meaning to life, became fixed in
my mind, and I saw that the only way to reach this reality
was by total detachment from the world. But I think that
even then I was aware of what Gandhi saw so clearly, that
this detachment was not a way of escape from the world but
of a freedom from self-interest which enabled one to give
oneself totally to God and to the world.

This was in accord with the lessons which I had to learn
gradually in the monastery during the following years.
Christian asceticism, like Indian, is based on detachment, a
radical separation from the world in order to give oneself
totally to God. But for a Christian this giving of oneself to
God necessarily means giving oneself to Christ – it is through
him that we come to the Father. But to give oneself to Christ
is to give oneself to all men, for he said: 'inasmuch as you
do it to the least of my brethren, you do it to me'. It is true
that in all spiritual life there is a certain tension between
these two aspects of the way. On the one hand there is the
need for a total renunciation, a denial of every created being,
in order to belong to God, the uncreated Being, alone, and
this can often lead to a separation from the world which
may seem to detach a man from all human society. But on the
other hand, both in Indian and in christian asceticism, one
can see a corresponding movement of concern for the world,
of the rediscovery of the world in God and of the service of
one's fellow men out of love for God. This is evident in both
the teaching and the example of the Buddha, but it was the
Bhagavad Gita which gave this view its classical expression.

* See below, p. 209 f.

The great message of the Gita was that God can be found not only by the way of the ascetic in silence and solitude, but also by the householder in his daily duties, if he makes the offering of everything he does to the Lord. It is this doctrine of selfless action, of working without seeking the 'fruit of work', that is of doing everything in a spirit of detachment from self and love for God, which inspired Mahatma Gandhi and made him give his life to the service of his fellow men in India. It is the same principle which has been at work in monastic life in the West, especially through the influence of the Rule of St Benedict. While the early Fathers of the Desert had been occupied, often exclusively, with the search for God alone, St Benedict, following on the example of St Basil, integrated the search for God with the life of the Church as a whole, that is with the social order, and thus the monks of St Benedict came to lay the foundations of civilization in the West. The life of prayer was co-ordinated with both manual and intellectual work and the monasteries became centres round which the economic and social life of the people was organized.

The result of this was that in medieval Europe the economic, social and political orders were all seen as subordinate in principle to the spiritual order, that is to the life of prayer and communion with God, and a hierarchy was thus established in which the life of every man from the serf to the feudal Lord could find its place. Now this was exactly the structure of society which we find in medieval India. Ancient Indian society was based, as is well known, on the four castes, or rather 'classes', for the four 'classes' were quite different from the multitude of castes, which afterwards developed. The classes consisted of the workers (the *Sudras*) at the basis, then the farmers and merchants (*Vaisyas*), then the warriors or rulers (*Kshetryas*) and finally at the top the Brahmins or priests. Here as in medieval Europe the priest, who is concerned with man's relation to God, the ultimate reality, was placed at the head of the social order, so that all human life and culture was integrated with religion.

This was further emphasized by the four *ashramas*, the four stages of life through which a man was expected to pass. The first was that of the student (*brahmachari* – literally the 'seeker of God'), whose principal study was the Vedas, the 'eternal law' (*sanatana dharma*) in which it was believed the source of all wisdom was to be found. Then came the stage of the householder, when a man married and brought up a family. But this in turn was seen as a preparation for a further stage, when, having fulfilled his duty to society, a man was expected to retire to the forest to meditate and prepare his soul for its release from this world, and finally for the last stage when, as a wandering Sannyasi, he renounced the world altogether to give himself to God alone. It is probable that this was always a more or less ideal scheme of life, but it bears witness to a profound understanding of the ultimate values of life. Ancient India did not neglect the values of this world, as it is sometimes imagined; it gave its due place to pleasure (*kama*), to wealth (*artha*) and above all to duty (*dharma* – the law by which each person fulfilled his function in society). But above all it placed 'liberation' (*moksha*), the 'release' from this world of space and time, the discovery of the ultimate reality, the being, knowledge and bliss (*sacchidananda*) in which the true meaning of life was to be found.

Thus ancient India, like medieval Europe, and we may add like ancient China and the islamic world, was a society in which the whole life of man was oriented towards the absolute, the ultimate truth to which everything in this world is relative. This is what gave such an astonishing stability to these societies, so that each of them was able to endure for a thousand years or more essentially unchanged. We are now witnessing the break-up of these great societies.

Even now the ancient order survives in many parts of
Europe and Asia but it is breaking up before the impact of
western civilization with increasing rapidity. In Europe the
break-up began with the Renaissance and was given a further
impetus with the Industrial Revolution and the French and
Russian revolutions. In China it began with the revolution
of Sun Yat Sen but the destruction of the old order has
been far more radical under communism. In India the
process may be said to have begun with the British but
since independence the rapidity of the change has increased
immeasurably. In the islamic world it began with Kemal
Ataturk in Turkey and is now spreading everywhere, and
it appears that nothing can long resist the impact of western
science and technology.

This is what constitutes the essential problem of the
modern world. We are in a stage of transition between the
break-up of the ancient cultures and the birth of a new
civilization. No one can doubt that modern civilization with
its science and technology, its democracy and humanism,
will prevail, but it becomes more and more clear that
modern civilization has no answer to give as to the ultimate
meaning of life. It has lost sight of the goal, which all the
ancient cultures held steadily before their eyes, and therefore
beneath all its external achievements there is a growing sense
of emptiness and of the meaninglessness of life. The problem
is, how are we to recover this sense of the absolute, of an
unconditioned to which we can commit ourselves, of an
ultimate meaning in the apparent meaninglessness of life?
The answer to this problem, it seems to me, can only come
through a meeting of East and West; neither can solve it by
itself. The structures of religion and society which prevailed
in the ancient world, whether in Europe or in Asia, are no
longer valid. A new structure has to be found and this will
necessarily be universal, as we now belong irrevocably to
one world. This means that a meeting must take place

between the different religions of the world. They can no
longer exist apart as they did in the past, each forming a
separate cultural unit. It is only when this meeting of
religions has taken place that an adequate spirituality will
be found for the needs of the modern world.

It is obvious that in this meeting of religions India will
have an important, if not a decisive, part to play. Not only
in view of its past history, which can boast of a spiritual
tradition second to none in the history of mankind, but also
in the light of its recent development, India has a natural
claim to spiritual leadership. In Ramakrishna, to whom more
than anyone Hinduism owes its revival in modern times; in
Mahatma Gandhi, who brought spiritual wisdom to bear
on political life as no one had done before him; and in Sri
Aurobindo and Ramana Maharshi,* in whom the philosophical and mystical genius of India lived on into the second
half of this century, India has brought forth men of spiritual
genius, to whom it would be difficult to find any parallel in
the West. So far, though Indian spirituality has been influenced by Christianity, orthodox Christianity has had practically no contact with the spiritual tradition of India. It is
this meeting between the orthodox tradition of Christianity
(whether Catholic, Orthodox or Protestant in form) and the
spiritual tradition of India (whether Hindu, Buddhist or
Jain) and also with Islam, especially in its mystical tradition
in which it stands to some extent between the two, which
seems to me to be the great need of the world today.

But this raises a particular problem. In India it is generally
assumed that all religions are essentially the same. They
differ in their 'rites and dogmas', that is in their external
forms of expression, but in their inward essence, that is
their ultimate significance, they are identical. There is one,
absolute, transcendent truth, which is manifested differently
in the different forms of religion. This 'transcendent unity'

* See below pp. 205, 213.

of religion has been compared to a white light, which is
broken up into different and apparently contrasting colours,
but which remains identical under all its forms. Or it can be
said that all religions are different paths to the same goal;
they all converge on the infinite, transcendent mystery in
which their true meaning is to be found. I believe that there
is a profound truth in this view, but it can easily be very
misleading. It is often suggested that the differences do not
really matter: they all disappear in the ultimate reality, which
transcends them. But I do not think that religious differences
can be so easily resolved. In christian belief there is an
essential truth, which is not relative but absolute, not
temporal but eternal and which must be preserved in any
genuine meeting of religions. Or rather, it may be said that
in Christianity it is precisely the relation between the relative
and the absolute, the temporal and the eternal, which is
essential. For a Christian the meeting of religions can only
take place in Christ, because in him is found the meeting
point of the relative and the absolute, of time and eternity,
of the one and the many, of God and man.

This poses the problem of the meeting of religions. How
is it possible to preserve the values of both East and West,
so that Christianity is not simply absorbed in Hinduism or
in eastern religion, and Hinduism and the other eastern
religions are not simply lost in Christianity? May we not
say that Christianity and western religion stand above all
for the reality of this world, of matter and man, of the
material world and human history? It is this that has enabled
the western world to make advances in the sphere of science
and technology, in the understanding of history and political
organization, beyond anything in the past. On the other
hand, the eastern world has always preserved the secret of
interiority, of an inner meaning behind this world of change.
It has never lost sight of the inner spirit, the Self, which is
present in all things and all men, which underlies and directs

the whole course of the material world and of human history. Often it has seemed to be prepared to renounce the phenomenal world altogether, to seek for nothing but a release from the conditions of space and time. Yet within the eastern tradition there has always been a certain realism which prevents it from going to this extreme, just as in the West there has always been a spiritual tradition, which recognizes a reality above this world and sees that the ultimate goal of mankind must be beyond this present world.

The meeting of religions must therefore consist in a new synthesis of these traditions. The East cannot renounce the advantages which have come to it through modern science and technology, through humanism and democracy, yet it must be able to integrate this new knowledge with its traditional wisdom. The West needs desperately to recover the spiritual tradition which it once possessed, and in doing so it must come into a living relation with eastern religion. Thus we may envisage a growing together of East and West, in which each will learn from the other, deepening their own tradition and integrating within it those new forces which are creating a new world today.

The essays in this book are all concerned with this problem of the meeting of religions in the setting of India. The background to them is the monastic life in which I have been engaged and which is described in the first three essays. My coming to India was due to my meeting with an Indian monk, whose lifelong desire it had been to introduce the monastic life into the Church in India. As there was then no monastery in India he had been professed as a monk in a European monastery, but was seeking for someone who would assist him in his enterprise. At first I saw no possibility of joining him, though I had already a deep love for India and a strong desire to go there. But in the course of time circumstances made it possible and I received permission to accompany him to Bangalore to assist in a monastic foundation.

Since my first encounter with the Dhammapada and the Bhagavad Gita my interest in eastern religion had grown steadily over the years. It was not merely an academic interest but rather a sense of need for that which Indian spirituality had to give. I had long been familiar with the mystical tradition of the West, but I felt the need of something more which the East alone could give; above all the sense of the presence of God in nature and the soul, a kind of natural mysticism which is the basis of all Indian spirituality. I felt therefore that if a genuine meeting of East and West was to take place, it must be at this deepest level of their experience and this I thought could best come through the monastic life. Europe has a long tradition of monastic life, beginning with St Antony of Egypt in the third century and spreading all over Palestine, Syria and Mesopotamia and westwards to Italy, France, Spain, Britain and Germany. Very little is known of this tradition in India because the early Catholic missionaries like Francis Xavier came from modern active orders, and British Protestantism had long ago rejected monasticism.

If the monastic life could be introduced into India, it would be something deeply congenial to the Indian mind. The ascetic tradition with its centre in the ashram is one of the most basic institutions of Indian life – Buddhist, Jain and Hindu. In modern times there has been a great revival of this ascetic tradition; not only the great mystics like Sri Aurobindo and Ramana Maharshi have centred their lives on the ashram, but a reformer like Mahatma Gandhi was led spontaneously from the beginning to base his life on an ashram. A remarkable development has also taken place of the Hindu ascetic ideal through the influence of the Ramakrishna Order, which Vivekananda founded to continue the work of his great master. Vivekananda introduced social work as an integral element in the monastic life, partly no doubt under christian influence, and this has brought Hindu

and christian monasticism much nearer together. The aim
of the monastic life remains always the 'search for God', or
for 'liberation' in Hindu terms, but through Mahatma
Gandhi and Vivekananda the search for God has come to
be intimately concerned with care for one's fellow-men.

Thus christian monasticism as conceived by Benedict
with its basic motive of seeking God in a life of prayer and
asceticism, but with its custom also of manual work and of
hospitality, which brought the monks into vital contact with
the life of their time, has a natural affinity with the ascetic
life as it is now conceived in India. It would seem that a
monastery offers an ideal setting for that meeting between
Christianity and Hinduism in which all that is most fundamental in each religion can find a place. If ancient India and
ancient Europe were both alike built up on the foundations
of monastic life, the goal of communion with God in prayer
being always maintained as the supreme purpose of life,
while economic and social life were seen as subordinate to
this end, might it not be that monasticism in the modern
world could bring that principle of spiritual order into life
which it has now lost? There can be no doubt that science
and technology, however necessary they may be, cannot
bring happiness by themselves, nor can they fulfil the deeper
needs of man. Unless a principle of spiritual order and integration can be introduced into the economic and social
development of Asia and Africa, there can be no hope of
stability and real progress.

Thus the monastery might come to be seen as a cell of
right living, where the proper relation of man with nature,
society and God may be worked out on a small scale, which
may serve as a model, as it did in times past. But this means
that in the monastery we have to recover the ancient sources
of spiritual life. For a Christian it means going back to the
sources of christian monasticism, not only in St Benedict,
but in the early Fathers of the Desert, who laid the found-

ations of monastic life in the East, in Egypt and Syria and
Mesopotamia. And in India it necessarily means also discovering the sources of Indian monasticism, the Upanishads
and the Bhagavad Gita and the different systems of Yoga.
Thus the meeting of eastern and western spirituality has to
take place in our own hearts first, and only then can we hope
to make a living contact with the Hindu and the Buddhist,
who likewise will be drawn to study christian monasticism.

When I first came out to India these ideas were only germ-
inating in my mind. In particular, at that time I had been
brought up in the Benedictine tradition and I thought that
the normal Benedictine life in the Latin rite, as it had come
down in the Middle Ages in Europe, was all that was required. We began, in fact, a monastery of this kind near
Bangalore soon after we arrived. We had a small bungalow
in modern style outside a village and we proceeded to furnish
it in what I thought was the greatest simplicity, with just a few
tables and chairs and beds and wash-stands. It was only after
we had been living there for some time that I discovered
that these were all unheard of luxuries in most of the houses
in the village, and only two or three of the richest people
possessed them. In the same way, we wore our monastic
habits with shoes and socks, but I realized after a time that
these also were an expensive luxury.

It became clear, therefore, that if we wanted to approach
the level of life not merely of the sannyasi, the monk, in
India, but even of the ordinary villager, a drastic change
would have to take place in our mode of life. But the experiment was valuable for many reasons. I was concerned above
all to make contact with Hinduism and Bangalore gave me
many opportunities. In the village where we were living
there were several university students, who soon began to
come up to see us. When they found that we had many
books on Indian life and philosophy, they were immediately
interested and began to come up regularly. In this way many

of them became our friends, and when I visited their houses
I was able to see something of living Hinduism. One of
them in particular became a very close friend, and to him I
have dedicated this book. I also met several of the university
professors and was able in this way to make contact with
modern Hindu thought. In all alike, both students and
professors, I found how deep was the influence of Hindu
tradition on their life and thought, in spite of their modern
education, and at the same time how open they were to
religious discussion.

An even more important event in some ways was my
discovery of the Hindu temple. When I first landed at
Bombay I went to see the Elephanta caves and the great
statue of Siva there left a lasting impression on me. Here at
the threshold of India I found graven in stone that profound
spirit of contemplation which has given its inner meaning
to all Indian life and thought. It is recollected in a deep re-
pose, like so many statues of the Buddha, revealing in stone
that awareness of the inner Spirit, the Atman, which to the
Hindu is the ground of all existence. When I went on to
visit the temples of Mysore and later the Tamil Nad, I discovered how the whole Hindu temple is a shrine of this
inner Spirit. The outer walls may be decorated with figures
of animals and men and gods, so that one is led by stages
through the different levels of life in this world, but in the
central shrine – the *garbha griha*, representing the 'cave of
the heart' – there may be nothing but a lingam, a bare stone
representing the formless divinity, the absolute godhead
which is beyond all 'name and form'.

The sexual origin of the lingam is, of course, obvious,
but this only brings out the extraordinary depth of understanding in ancient India. Sex was always regarded as something 'holy' – I think that it still is, except where the Indian
spirit has been corrupted by the West. The lingam was
therefore a natural symbol of the sacred 'source of life'. But

with the profound metaphysical sense of ancient India this source of life was inevitably seen not as a mere biological reality but as the absolute Being, the eternal reality which is life and consciousness and bliss – the infinite, formless *sacchidananda*. I remember once sitting down by the river by the side of a little shrine in which I found there was nothing but a roughly carved lingam and yoni (the male and female organs). The natural reaction of a European is to think that this is something 'obscene'; but to me it seemed a touching expression of the sense of the 'sacred', the awareness of the essential holiness of nature and of faith in her generative powers.

Perhaps this is the deepest impression left by life in India, the sense of the sacred as something pervading the whole order of nature. Every hill and tree and river is holy, and the simplest human acts of eating and drinking, still more of birth and marriage, have all retained their sacred character. It is this that gives such an indescribable beauty to Indian life, in spite of the poverty and squalor. Wealth and sanitation are of little value if this sense of the sacred is to be lost in the process. Perhaps there is nothing which the western world needs more urgently to recover than this sense of the sacred. In the West everything has become 'profane'; it has been deliberately emptied of all religious meaning. In part this was an inevitable reaction to the 'sacred order' of the Middle Ages, by which people were driven to concentrate more and more on secular and human values to the exclusion of religion. Yet now that the economic and social and political orders have won their independence, they need to recover a religious basis if human life is not to be emptied of all ultimate meaning. It is here that the West needs to learn from the East the sense of the 'holy', of a transcendent mystery which is immanent in everything and which gives an ultimate meaning to life.

This Hindu sense of the sacred was wonderfully illustrated

for me one day when I was living near Bangalore. I was visiting a little temple to the monkey-god Hanuman, the faithful companion of Rama in the story of the Ramayana, which was a short distance from our monastery. As I was coming away I met an old Brahmin, who spoke good English and had, in fact, been educated in a christian school. He no doubt wondered what I would make of a monkey-god and began to explain to me that God is manifested in every form in the universe, whether in plant or animal or man; it is therefore possible to worship God, the one infinite, eternal Being, under the form of a monkey, as in that of a tree or a man. But above all, he went on to say, God is present in the human heart, and he quoted some stanzas of the Bhagavad Gita in Sanskrit in the rhythmical chant which is used in the recitation of Sanskrit. This was a wonderful example to me of the deep roots of Hindu tradition, the sense of the one eternal Spirit pervading the universe and manifested in everything, which has been enshrined in the doctrine of the Upanishads and the Bhagavad Gita, and come down into the life of the ordinary villager today. In this sense it is difficult to speak of either polytheism or idolatry in Hinduism; for to the Hindu every god is but a manifestation of the one, eternal absolute Being and every idol is but the sacramental presence of the one infinite Spirit.

In the end it proved impossible to make a foundation in Bangalore and we moved to Kerala at the extreme south-west tip of India. There we joined with Father Francis Mahieu, a Cistercian, who had come out to India with the same purpose, and eventually a monastery was established there. I have described this monastery in the first chapter of this book. It involved a new beginning in two important ways. In the first place, we adopted the Syrian instead of the Latin rite, as the majority of Christians in Kerala belong to the Syrian Church. This immediately opened to us the whole world of eastern Christianity, of which I had known little until then. Most people think of Christianity as an essentially western religion, as it has largely become. But the Syrian Church is there to remind us that before the Church spoke Greek or Latin it spoke Aramaic, and while it was extending westwards to Greece and Rome, it was also extending eastwards through Palestine and Syria to Mesopotamia. Both Greek and Latin Christianity remain essentially western in their style and habit of thought, though Greek Christianity certainly underwent a strong oriental influence. But the Syrian Church is essentially eastern; it belongs to the Middle East and bears everywhere on it the marks of its origin. It was in this form that Christianity spread eastwards in the succeeding centuries to China and India, and it is in this form that it seems to be most naturally adapted to the peoples of the East.

Yet the Syrian Church belongs strictly to the Middle East; it is still very far from the culture of the Far East. At most it can serve as a bridge by which Christianity may eventually be adapted to the culture of India, China and Japan. The great task of the Church in the Far East must always be to enter fully into the cultural inheritance of these peoples. It is true that there remains a judaic core at the heart of Christianity which it can never abandon. It is rooted in the traditions of the semitic world from which it sprang, and this semitic basis must always remain both in the liturgy and in the life and thought of the Church. On this basis the Greek and Latin churches, and later the various Protestant churches built up their own ways of life and thought. In the Far East this basis must inevitably remain, but instead of western habits of life and thought the Church has to build up an Indian, a Chinese, a Japanese Christianity.

The general use of the vernacular in the liturgy has now made possible a beginning in this direction, but this is only a first step. The great need is to have a theology constructed

on the basis of Indian and Chinese thought, and beyond
that a christian spirituality, which will draw on all the
infinite resources of eastern spirituality, Hindu, Buddhist,
Taoist and Confucian. This is a task which has hardly been
begun. In India we need a christian Vedanta and a christian
Yoga, that is a system of theology which makes use not
only of the terms and concepts but of the whole structure
of thought of the Vedanta, as the Greek Fathers used Plato
and Aristotle; and a spirituality which will make use not
merely of the practices of Hatha Yoga, by which most people
understand Yoga, but of the great systems of Karma, Bhakti
and Jnana Yoga, the way of works or action, of love or
devotion, and of knowledge or wisdom, through which the
spiritual genius of India has been revealed through the
centuries.

It is here in the sphere of spirituality that a monastery or
ashram has above all its part to play. A monastery must
always be concerned with the 'search for God', the continual
effort to 'realize' God, to discover the reality of the hidden
presence of God in the depths of the soul. It is the task of
the christian monk to try to enter into the whole tradition
of Indian *Sannyasa*, the renunciation of the world and all
family ties in order to 'realize' God, to discover the indwelling presence of God both in nature and in the soul.
No mere external asceticism and no merely theoretical knowledge of God in the Hindu view is of any value unless it
leads to the actual experience of God as a Being more real
than nature or the soul, without whom neither nature nor the
soul has any reality. This is the point at which Hindu and
christian spirituality have to meet. We have to make the
discovery of Christ as the Atman, the true Self, of every
being. For 'in him', says St Paul, 'everything in heaven and
earth was created . . . the whole universe has been created
in him and for him, and he exists before everything and
all things are held together in him'; and St John says: 'he is

the true light which enlightens every man coming into the world'.

It is this experience of Christ as the ground of all being which must be the inspiration of a christian monasticism. For this means that in Christ we not only discover the centre or ground of our being, but we also find a meeting point with all other men and with the whole world of nature. There is a necessary separation from the world in a monastic life, a discipline of silence and solitude which is necessary for the discovery of this inner centre of our being. But this separation should not divide a monk from the world but on the contrary enable him to meet the world at the deepest level of its being. 'A monk is one who separates himself from all men in order that he may be united with all men', was one of the sayings of the monastic fathers. It is at this point that the meeting of religions must ultimately take place. For here just as there is neither 'Jew nor Greek', so there is neither Hindu nor Buddhist, neither Muslim nor Parsee, but all are one in Christ.

It is at this point also that the life of a monk is integrated with the life of the world. To meet another man in Christ is necessarily to be concerned with his whole being, body and soul. Here in India, in particular, it is impossible not to be concerned constantly with the problem of poverty. We are surrounded here by people who are living at the bare level of subsistence, and in constant danger of falling below it. I was taken once to a village where I was told that the people could at best get one meal a day, and at certain seasons would get no more than one meal in two or three days. Yet there is another side to this picture. My informant, who knew his people well, told me that he had never found so much faith and trust in God as he found among those villagers. They were partly Hindu and partly christian, but all alike had the same faith in God and capacity for cheerful and patient endurance. The danger in India today is that this aspect of

things should be forgotten. The need for raising the standard
of living is so great that it tends to occupy all the attention.

But economic and social improvement with the education
that goes with them can bring no real and lasting happiness
unless they are integrated with the spiritual life of the people.
Often they tend simply to disintegrate the life of the village,
not only undermining religious faith but also breaking up
the bonds of love and affection which bind people together
in hard times. In a poor village there is often an extraordinarily close bond of sympathy existing between the
villagers and a spirit of co-operation whenever anyone is in
need. I once asked a friend who came from a village himself
and knew his people intimately, what was the real religion
of the villagers, and he replied: Oh their religion is love!
There is no doubt about the need to raise the standard of
living, but this has to be part of an integrated plan, in which
the social, moral and religious life of the people is developed
along with their economic condition and their general
education.

It was this that led me to take an interest in the *Sarvodaya*
movement of Vinoba Bhave.* Vinoba has gone all over India,
walking from village to village, trying to get the rich to
give land to the poor and to awaken a spirit of co-operation
in the villages. Practically, it must be said, that, though he
has collected millions of acres of land, his organization is
very defective and actual change in the condition of life in
the villages is very slow. And yet his movement has an
immense significance, because he is not concerned simply
with standards of life, but with a new order of society, a
new way of life altogether. The *Sarvodaya* movement was
begun by Mahatma Gandhi and its inspiration is to be found
in the deepest principles of Hindu thought. Gandhi based
his life work, as is well known, on two principles – truth

* See especially chap. 10.

(*satya*) and non-violence (*ahimsa*). By truth he meant adher-
ence to the inner principle of Being, the Atman or Spirit,
which governs the universe, and by non-violence he meant
far more than a negative ideal, but rather the basic respect
for every man as an image of God, in whom the universal
Spirit dwells. Vinoba's principles are exactly the same.

Thus the *Sarvodaya* movement has a spiritual basis which
is in accordance with the best traditions of Hinduism. The
economic and social reform which it seeks to introduce is
seen essentially as a means for men to 'realize' themselves as
human beings, and this in Hindu thought necessarily means
the realization of their fundamental relation to God, the
ground of all being. What is perhaps rather new in Hinduism
is the insistence that this can only come about through the
realization of man's essential relation to his neighbour and
to the land on which he depends for his livelihood. All distinction of caste is abolished and the land is conceived as
belonging to the people as a whole, to be worked on a basis
of co-operation. Here surely is another point of meeting
between the Hindu and the christian ideal. The happiness
of man can ultimately only be found when he finds once
more the right relationship with God and nature and his
fellow men.

The christian ideal of social and economic life has been
pictured for ever in the Acts of the Apostles, where we read
that the disciples were 'of one heart and soul, and none of
them called any of his possessions his own, but they had all
things in common'. This experiment in christian communism appears to have been short-lived, but it has remained
as an ideal within the Church always present in the monastic
and religious life. The significance of the *Sarvodaya* movement is that it aims at extending this ideal to the whole
people and eventually to the whole world. One may think
that this aim is utopian, especially if the ideal of all land
being held in common is taken literally, yet it points to an

ideal of human society which neither capitalism nor communism can satisfy. Capitalism, by concentrating on the
freedom of the individual, leads to a competitive form of
society and to the exploitation of man and nature which
bears within it the seeds of disintegration, however much it
may be corrected by the aims of social justice. Communism,
while endeavouring to correct the evils of capitalism, sup-
presses the freedom of the individual and leads to forcible
collectivization. The ideal of Mahatma Gandhi and Vinoba
Bhave stands in between the two. It rejects the violence
implicit in both capitalism and communism and seeks to
establish a human society on the basis of *ahimsa*, that is of a
non-violence which respects the freedom of the individual
and yet seeks for a co-operative order of society, in which
the individual freely surrenders his right to private ownership for the common good.

These ideals may seem remote from christian society at
the present time, yet they have a firm basis not only in the
gospel but also in the teaching and practice of the early
Church. The ideal of common ownership was stronger in the
early Church than we are generally inclined to believe and
several of the Fathers maintained that all land was originally held in common, and that private ownership only came
in as a result of sin. In the same way, we are realizing that
pacifism was common teaching in the early Church, the use
of arms being considered unworthy of a Christian. The early
Fathers took literally the prophecies of the messianic age,
that 'they shall beat their swords into plowshares and their
spears into pruning hooks' and considered that Christ had
put an end to war. It was the Peace of Constantine, which
led to so many evils in the Church, which prepared the way
for the christian acceptance of war and violence as a means
for advancing the common good.

This would seem therefore to be a point at which Hindu
and christian ideals can again meet. The Christian can learn

from the Hindu to take the Sermon on the Mount more
seriously and the Hindu can perhaps learn from the Christian
a greater degree of realism in the conception both of the
practice of non-violence and of communal ownership. Non-
violence cannot be practised indiscriminately, as Gandhi
himself realized; it demands a concentrated moral training
and a conquest of self, for which few in practice are prepared.
In the same way, though the principle of common ownership
may be accepted, in the sense that the land belongs to the
people as a whole, yet in practice it is rather by different
forms of co-operation that the land and other material resources can be developed than by strict communism.

Yet we must always remember that the economic and
social order depend ultimately on the religious order. Unless
the life of man is ordered from beginning to end on a right
relation with God, the ultimate ground of all existence,
there can never be any real stability. In this matter it should
be possible to realize some form of co-operation between
all the different religious traditions. Hinduism, Buddhism,
Judaism, Islam and Christianity, all alike share certain social
and economic ideals, based on the right relation between
man and nature and God, which are being threatened by
modern civilization. If they could find a common basis on
which to work together, then they would exercise an incalculable influence on the world. It would then be possible
to conceive a new world order, in which the ideals of modern
science and technology, of humanism and democracy could
be integrated in a spiritual order, which would give them
that relation to ultimate truth and reality which they need.

In August 1963 I was invited to speak on the meeting of
East and West at an ecumenical conference at Santa Fé in
New Mexico. The talks which I gave there and at New York
and the following essays in this book are all concerned with
this fundamental problem of the meeting of religions in the

modern world. Since then the establishment of a Secretariat
for non-Christian Religions in Rome has given a new direction to this discussion within the Catholic Church. We are
now committed to an ecumenical approach to other religions
parallel to that with other christian Churches. The lines of
this approach have yet to be worked out, but it seems clear
that they must proceed like those among Christians by discovering first what are the common principles which all
religions hold in common, especially in the moral order,
and then seeking ways of co-operation in practical affairs,
especially the building up of economic and social life in the
countries of Asia and Africa. But behind this there remains
the more serious problem of how we are to envisage the
relation of these religions to one another. It is clear that we
can no longer take a negative view, each religion either
ignoring the others or regarding them as enemies.

Yet when we try to establish a positive relation between
the different religions we immediately encounter great diffi-
culties. This arises primarily from the conflict between the
semitic group of religions, Judaism, Islam and Christianity,
on the one hand, and the oriental religions, especially
Hinduism and Buddhism, on the other. For the Hindu,
there is no problem. There is one, absolute, infinite, eternal
Being, the Brahman, which is manifested in all the different
forms of nature and human life. The object of life is to
realize the absolute, indivisible unity of this one Being, not
merely mentally but spiritually, so that one discovers in the
depths of one's being an identity with this one Absolute.
When this identity becomes known, then all differences disappear; the absolute, simple identity of all being is ex-
perienced in an ecstasy of pure bliss. This is *moksha*, liberation, which may be attained even in this world, and must
be attained eventually by all beings in the course of rebirth.

In the Hindu view all religions are but different paths towards this one goal. In the course of history there has been

a succession of 'great souls', who have attained to this knowledge of the supreme identity and have been able to map
out the path of realization for others. Among these 'great
souls', whom Hindus would not hesitate to call 'incarnations'
of God, would be included not only Rama and Krishna, the
heroes of the Hindu epics, but also the Buddha, Christ and
Mohammed, and also spiritual leaders of modern times like
Ramakrishna and Ramana Maharshi. Such a view is all-
embracing and answers the problem of religion from a
Hindu point of view to perfection. But this unity of religion
is won at a cost that no orthodox Christian or Muslim or
Jew will admit. For it means that there is ultimately no
difference between God and man and nature; all distinctions
disappear in the one absolute Being. This means that ultimately the world and time and history are unreal; their
appearance is an effect of 'ignorance' (*avidya*) and when
known for what they are, they disappear like the form of
the snake which has been mistakenly superimposed on a
rope.

Against this view the Jew, the Christian and the Muslim
maintain the absolute transcendent reality of the one God,
the creator of heaven and earth, who creates man in his own
image and likeness and calls him to share in his own bliss,
but can never be identified with him. Man and nature are
creatures of God; they have a real being, dependent on God
but really distinct from him, a relative being, which is inconceivable apart from God the absolute Being, but can
never become the absolute. Further, the semitic religions
maintain that man is separated from God not merely by an
illusion of the mind, by 'ignorance', as in Hinduism, but by
sin, that is by an aversion from the will of God, the absolute
Good. Sin is not an illusion which can be dispelled by knowledge but a fault in our nature for which atonement has to
be made. It can be seen from this how the semitic religions
offer a far better ground for realism. The world and nature

are real; man and history have a meaning and a purpose in
the mind of God. The divine action in the world is not
merely an appearance of the one, eternal Being, but an action
of God in history which gives an ultimate meaning to human
life. Time does not move in a cycle of rebirths as for the
Hindu, but in a straight line towards a goal which is set before both the individual and the race.

It would seem that in this doctrine of the one, supreme
personal God, who is infinitely holy and just and good and
yet infinitely merciful; of a world which is created by God
in total dependence on him and yet really distinct from him,
which is the sphere of both good and evil forces; and the
conception of history as having a purpose, determined by
God, according to which the whole creation is moving towards a definite end, when it will be judged by God and the
good separated from the evil; we have a unique revelation,
made originally to the Jews, on which both Christianity and
Islam depend. This conception gives a reality to nature and
history, and therefore to science and political life, which is
lacking in Hindu and Buddhist thought, and which is better
adapted to the modern world. It was in fact from this semitic
tradition that the whole modern movement of science and
humanism, of democracy and technology, arose, and it is
difficult to see how the world can go back on what has been
gained in this way.

On the other hand, both the semitic religions and the
modern world have a great deal to learn from Hinduism.
There is always the danger of a personal God being conceived in too human terms and becoming an idol, an image
of a glorified man. The problems raised in the Bishop of
Woolwich's *Honest to God* and in the theology of Tillich
and Bonhoeffer are evidence of this. Against this the Hindu
conception of the Brahman, the one, infinite, eternal Being,
beyond speech and thought, of whom we can ultimately say
no more than 'neti, neti', because the divine being transcends

every image and conception of human thought, is of enduring value. Further, if when we speak of the person of God, we mean a being of infinite wisdom and goodness, yet we have to admit that all these terms of person, being, wisdom and goodness, can only be used by analogy, so that God in himself infinitely transcends all that we can conceive of him. Thus we are not far from the Hindu conception of the Brahman as *Sacchidananda*, Being, Knowledge, Bliss, who is yet beyond conception. Only we have to insist that in this Being of infinite mystery, the attributes of personal being really exist and are not mere appearances, so that we can properly speak of personal relations, that is relations of knowledge and love within the absolute Being of the Godhead, according to the christian doctrine of the trinity, as well as of personal relations between God and man.

Again if we insist on the reality of the creation as distinct from God, so that the world is in no sense either an illusion or a modification of the Being of God, yet we have also to admit that creation itself is a mystery, that is to say that it properly transcends human understanding. We know that the world exists in a relative, temporal-spatial mode of being, and that God exists absolutely in an infinite and eternal mode, but we cannot properly grasp the relation between the two. Thus the Hindu doctrine of Maya is not without significance, and it would appear that Sankara in particular was actually feeling his way towards a theory of creation. There are also the more realist doctrines in Hinduism of Dvaita (dualist) philosophy and of the Saiva Siddhanta which come nearer to the semitic conception. Thus both in the conception of God and in that of creation the way is open to a deeper understanding which could bring the semitic and oriental religions closer to each other.

Finally in regard to the conception of the end of man, the two systems may not be so far apart as appears. It is difficult to fit the Hindu and Buddhist conception of *Samsara*, of rebirth, into any system of Jewish-christian thought, but if we consider that all mankind ultimately forms one organic whole, so that individuals do not exist as isolated units, but are all members of one body, which is in the course of growth throughout human history, and is further linked organically with the evolution of the universe, then it may be possible to give a meaning to *karma* and transmigration, especially if we remember Sankara's saying that 'the Lord is the only Transmigrator'. We can then conceive of this body of humanity, evolving throughout history, as the sphere of the divine action which is gradually leading it out of its fallen state of sin into its ultimate state of blissful participation in the divine life. Indications of this conception can be found in the Hindu doctrine of Purusha, the supreme Person, who is manifested in all the different forms of human life; in the Buddhist doctrine of the Buddha-nature, which is hidden in all men and waits to be manifested; in the jewish conception of Adam Qadmon, the first man, in whom the whole of mankind is summed up, and in the islamic doctrine of the universal man, in whom not only human nature but the whole universe finds its archetype.

It is not difficult to see how this harmonizes with the christian doctrine of the mystical body of Christ, who is called by St Paul the second Adam. In this view Christ is seen as the eternal Logos, the Word in whom all things exist, who assumes the whole of mankind, and with mankind the whole of nature, to himself and makes of them one body. The sin which has separated both nature and man from God is undone, and through the cross of Christ nature and man are once more reconciled with God. Can we not see how in this the Logos of St John is related to the Purusha or the Atman of Hinduism, the *Dharmakaya* or 'divine body' of Mahayana Buddhism, the wisdom of Hebrew tradition and the universal man of Islam? In him is fulfilled the idea which underlies all these traditions and we can speak of something like a universal witness to the mystery of Christ. The christian affirmation is simply that this mystery which was hidden in each of the great religions was manifested historically in the life and death and resurrection of Jesus Christ.

But if we believe that Christ thus assumed the whole order of nature and of mankind to himself, we believe that in so doing he raised both alike to a participation in the divine nature. In this the true end and purpose of the whole creation is revealed; nature and man are to be raised to a participation in the divine nature, that is in the divine mode of being. It is here that we can see the link between the christian and Hindu conceptions of the last end of man. Hinduism has always understood that the end of man is to share in the divine life, in the divine being, knowledge and bliss. That is to say man, and with him nature which is as it were his body, is to participate in the divine mode of knowledge or consciousness, which is essentially 'non-dual'. The divine nature is absolutely simple; in it being, knowing and willing are one identical act, and every attribute of God, such as wisdom, goodness, beauty, truth, is identical with the divine being itself. Further, in knowing man and the universe God knows them as aspects of his own being, which in him are identified with his own essence. Man and an animal in God, as Eckhart said, are God; there is an identity between the 'ideas' of God, as Aquinas explained, and the divine essence.

If then man is to share in the divine nature, in the divine mode of knowledge, it must mean that man will share in this non-dual mode of knowledge. He will know himself and all things in their 'ideas' in God, that is in their identity with the divine nature. This is surely the profound truth towards which the whole doctrine of *advaita* aspires. It was an intuition, grasped already in the Upanishads and made the

basis of all Hindu philosophy, by which India has been led
throughout her history in her quest for the knowledge of
God. It can be seen therefore how close the Hindu, and
with it the Buddhist and islamic Sufi conception of the
ultimate state of man comes to the christian. The difference
lies in this. For the Hindu and the Buddhist, as for certain
currents in islamic thought, in the ultimate state there is an
absolute identity. Man realizes his identity with the absolute
and realizes that this identity is eternal and unchangeable.
In the christian view man remains distinct from God. He is
a creature of God, and his being raised to a participation in
the divine life is an act of God's grace, a gratuitous act of
infinite love, by which God descends to man in order to
raise him to share in his own life and knowledge and love.
In this union man truly shares in the divine mode of knowledge, he knows himself in an identity with God, but he
remains distinct in his being. It is an identity, or rather a
communion, by knowledge and love, not an identity of being.

The differences between the two views cannot be denied.
They are profound and far-reaching and affect the whole life
of man. Yet at the same time we can see how close they
come together, how they show a profound affinity, which
indicates the movement of a common spirit among them.
We have surely the right to speak of a common tradition
among the different religious traditions, often obscured and
often appearing in a contradictory form, but witnessing to
a common origin and a common goal. As the different
religions draw nearer to one another in mutual respect,
seeking the ultimate truth to which they all alike bear witness, may we not hope that they may eventually arrive at
unity? Yet perhaps we have to allow that this ultimate unity
will only be reached at the end of time. It is notable that all
the different religions look forward to a figure who is to
appear at the end of time. The Hindus expect the last *avatara*
in the form of Kalki, the Buddhists await the coming of the

Buddha Maitreya, the Jews look for the coming of the Messiah, and both Christians and Muslims expect the coming of Jesus, though of course the significance of it for them is not the same.

In all these figures we can see an indication of the mystery of the end of man, the expectation of something yet to come by which our present state of being will be brought to an end and the ultimate truth will be revealed. Before we can reach this state we have to pass beyond this world of space and time, beyond all the images and concepts of our mind, and it is in that darkness which is beyond all light, in that Nirvana where the light of this world is 'blown out', which Mahayana Buddhism speaks of as *Sunya*, or the void, that the ultimate mystery of truth will be revealed. Perhaps it is only in that ultimate state of knowledge, when we 'shall know even as we are known', that the different religions will find their supreme point of unity. While we remain in this world of shadows and images, where the truth is always hidden under a veil, we have each to follow the light of truth which is given us, while we strive to open our minds to that truth wherever it may be found, confident that truth cannot contradict itself, even though its final reconciliation may not be found in this world.

BEDE GRIFFITHS
Kurisumala Ashram, 1965

PART ONE

Towards an Indian Monasticism

1. Kurisumala Ashram

KURISUMALA ASHRAM is a monastery of the Syrian Rite in South India. It owes its origin to two monks, one a Cistercian and the other a Benedictine, who came to India in 1955, and after some experiments in monastic life apart, joined together in 1958 to found a contemplative monastery in Kerala. The monastery takes its name from Kurisumala, the 'hill of the cross', a mountain among the high ranges of Kerala, below which the monastery lies. It is in a beautiful position, looking over the hills to Anamudi, the highest peak in South India (9,000 ft) on one side, and over the foothills and the plain to the sea on another. It is a wild and solitary place, not long ago the haunt of elephant and bison, but now joined to the plain by a new road which has been cut through the hills.

As the Syrian Church in Kerala represents an eastern tradition which has become adapted to the Indian way of life, it was decided to found the monastery in the Syrian rite. But for this purpose the West Syrian rite of Antioch was chosen, which is used by the Jacobites, rather than the Chaldean rite, which is that of the majority of Catholics and has been in use for a much longer time. The rite of Antioch was introduced into the Catholic Church in India in 1930, when Mar Ivanios, one of the Jacobite bishops, was reunited with Rome, bringing another bishop and a considerable number of priests and laity with him. This rite has the advantage of being a pure oriental rite, which has not suffered from latinization like the Chaldean rite. At the same time it was felt that this rite would be a valuable means of an ecumenical

approach to the Jacobites and of working for the reunion of
the separated Syrian Christians.

Thus the monastery was given an ecumenical character
from the beginning. But it was felt that in India it is necessary
for an ecumenical movement to extend beyond the reunion
of Christians and to embrace also the Hindus. For this reason
it was decided to adopt the *kavi* (saffron-coloured) habit of
the Indian sannyasi and to follow as far as possible the
customs of a Hindu ashram. The tradition of *sannyasa*, or renunciation of the world, goes back to the earliest period of
Indian history and the kavi habit is common to both the
Buddhist and the Hindu ascetic. It remains a living tradition
in India today and there are thousands of ashrams scattered
all over the country. It was our desire to enter into this
tradition of Indian *sannyasa* and to establish a christian ashram, in which the life of prayer and asceticism could be
followed along christian lines, yet keeping always in touch
with the traditions of India.

As there is practically no living tradition of monasticism
in the Syrian Church today, we decided to follow the Rule
of St Benedict with a strict Cistercian observance, so as to
emphasize the note of prayer and asceticism in our life. But
from the beginning we were drawn to the ancient tradition
of oriental monasticism, both of Syria and of Egypt, which
was the source of western monasticism. The Syrian liturgy
naturally assisted our development along these lines, but we
also make use of the Syrian fathers. Canonically the monastery is an eastern monastery of 'eparchial' rank, that is,
coming under the jurisdiction of the bishop and subject to
oriental canon law. In an eastern monastery according to
tradition there is no specific 'rule'. Each monastery has a
typikon, a rule of life based on the teaching of the Fathers,
which it is free to adapt to its own needs. We are thus able
to make use not only of the Rule of St Benedict, but also of
the Rules of Syrian monasticism like that of Abraham of

Kaskar, of the great monastery near Nisibis in the sixth century. Basically this means that we have been led not so much to adopt any particular rule of life as to try to recover the significance of the original monastic tradition, the 'monastic order', which existed before there were any particular orders in the Church. This has meant first of all a return to the bible, on which the whole monastic tradition is based, but to the bible interpreted in the light of the patristic tradition. In this respect the Syrian liturgy has been of decisive importance. It is a semitic liturgy, owing something to the Greek, but essentially semitic in its style and mode of thought. The divine office makes comparatively little use of the psalms but is largely made up of original compositions in verse based on the tradition established by St Ephrem in the fourth century. These compositions are of great variety and beauty and are nearly always profoundly biblical. They are often meditations based on biblical themes, but bringing out the mystical and symbolic sense of the scriptures and thus giving an initiation into a biblical theology. The theme of Adam and paradise, of the fall and redemption through Christ's descent into Sheol to raise up Adam and restore him to paradise is one of the basic themes, so also is that of the resurrection, the expectation of the dead in Sheol and the second coming of Christ. Thus the liturgy is set in the mould of the primitive christian tradition especially that of Jewish-christian thought, which Père Daniélou has studied in his book on the theology of Jewish Christianity.

There are also regular readings from the bible in the Syrian liturgy on Sundays and feast days, both from the Old and the New Testament. Here again the typical sense of the Old Testament is brought out very strongly and this reinforces the lesson of the liturgy. Thus the bible and liturgy together form the basis of the spiritual life of the ashram. But to these are added the eastern Fathers, Cassian's

Conferences and the *Lives of the Fathers* as recommended by
St Benedict, but also the Syrian Fathers as found in the
Philokalia, and especially the works of St Isaac of Niniveh.
The main themes of this tradition are first of all 'repentance',
that is *metanoia*, the change of heart, which is seen as the
fundamental disposition of the christian life, and 'perpetual
prayer', the constant 'prayer of the heart', considered as the
goal to be sought. This gives the whole life a deeply contemplative character. It has been found of great assistance
for this purpose to have a short period of silent prayer at
the end of each office, and of each nocturne during Lilio,
the night office. This prevents the recitation of the office becoming mechanical and gives an opportunity for developing
the habit of contemplative prayer.

Though the technique of the hesychast 'prayer of Jesus'*
is not necessarily used, the basic principles of this method
of prayer can be accepted. Whether the repetition of the
divine name or the formula of invocation, 'Lord Jesus
Christ, Son of God, have mercy on me a sinner', together
with the practice of regular breathing are used or not, the
essence of this prayer consists in the recollection of the
thoughts in the 'place of the heart' and through this the
experience of the indwelling presence of the Holy Spirit. It
is obvious that this method of prayer has much in common
with the Hindu system of Yoga, in which deep breathing
and the repetition of the divine name are used to assist a
deep recollection of the mind and senses, leading to *samadhi*,
the absorption of the mind in God, that is the Brahman.
There is, it is true, a fundamental difference in the Hindu
and the christian experience, in that the one is an experience
of 'identity', the other of 'communion', but it is at this point
of interior prayer above all that the contact between Hindu
and Christian has to be made.

Our other contacts with Hindu tradition are rather in

* See below, p. 207 f.

external customs. We follow the tradition of Hindu sannyasis by wearing the 'kavi' habit, kavi being the sacred colour in India, by going barefoot, sitting on the floor, eating with our hands and sleeping on mats. These are all traditional customs not only of sannyasis but of normal life in ancient India; so also is the custom of doing without practically any furniture. The food is according to Hindu custom strictly vegetarian, consisting of rice and vegetables and fruit, with milk and *ghee*, or purified butter. All this not only keeps us in touch with Hindu tradition but also helps us not to be too far removed from the poverty of the ordinary Indian villager. This external poverty is considered to be an essential mark of 'holiness' in India and there is no doubt that it makes a deep impression on a Hindu. We have found that government officials, who may themselves follow a European way of life, have a great respect nevertheless for such a life of poverty, prayer and penance.

In order to support ourselves we run a dairy farm, which we hope to raise to the number of fifty milking cows. This has been a means of bringing us into contact with the local people as well as with government officials. We agreed to import two Jersey bulls from England to be used in the insemination of all the cattle in this area, and the government in return agreed to set up a 'key village centre' here with a veterinary staff. This means that we take our part in the great 'community development' plan for all India and at the same time get the assistance of expert advice whenever it is needed. It is hoped that this will lead in time to the development of the whole of this area as a dairy centre for Kerala. Thus without involving ourselves in any external activity we are able to enter fully into the life of the people around us, who are mostly very poor.

The community now numbers fifteen, with three priests including one Indian father who has joined us, and twelve brothers, of whom four have made their solemn profession

and five are due to make their profession this year. It can
therefore be said that the community has become firmly
established and has begun to take root in the country. It is
only a small beginning, yet we feel that it has the possibilities
of growth. The most important task is, of course, to establish
the contemplative life on a firm basis and this will take many
years, but we have at the same time been able to make many
ecumenical contacts. It began with a meeting some years
ago, when the news of the summoning of the Vatican
Council was first announced. Since that time, with the
growth of the new ecumenical understanding fostered by
the Vatican Council and the World Council of Churches,
the movement has steadily grown and we have established
good relations with the bishops, priests and people of all the
different churches.

Contacts with Hindus on a deeper level than the social
are not so easy, but we have had at least one meeting between Christians and Hindus to discuss the nature of ultimate truth, which proved to be most encouraging. It is
hoped that in time it will be possible to have more Hindus
visit us and to enter into a genuine dialogue with them. This
demands on our part an ever deeper understanding of the
Hindu point of view and at the same time a clear grasp of
the fundamental difference in the christian point of view.
The danger in the encounter with Hinduism is always that
of a superficial syncretism, which would regard all religions
as 'essentially' the same, and only differing in their 'accidental'
characteristics. Needless to say, this is destructive of all
serious dialogue and makes real understanding impossible.

What is required is a meeting of the different religious
traditions at the deepest level of their experience of God.
Hinduism is based on a deep mystical experience and everywhere seeks not simply to know 'about' God, but to 'know
God', that is to experience the reality of God in the depths of
the soul. It is at this level that Christian and Hindu have to

meet, to discover in their experience of God, what is really common and where the real differences arise. It is here that we believe that a monastery can play a decisive part. It should be the work of the monk by the practice of prayer and contemplation to enter ever more deeply into the experience of God to seek for an even closer union with God in the depths of the soul. Such an experience will lead him to understand the Hindu mystical experience, as it were from within. But at the same time, as his contemplation is centred on Christ, it will lead not to that experience of 'identity', which is the tendency of all Hindu mysticism, but to the experience of 'communion', with Christ, and through Christ with the persons of the holy Trinity and with other persons in the mystical body of Christ. It is from this fundamental christian experience that he has to move out to meet his brethren in other religions and to seek to understand them. It is this witness to Christ, through a life lived in intimate union with him, which we believe to be the work of the monk in India, and perhaps there is no more important work in India today. Ultimately a Hindu will not be convinced by arguments, but by a life lived in the closest intimacy with God.

2. Kerala

KERALA IS the name given in the reorganization of the states in the Republic of India, to what was before composed of the three states of Travancore, Cochin and Malabar. It is a narrow strip of land in the extreme south-west, consisting of a coastal region about thirty miles broad interlaced with backwaters and canals and covered with coconut palms, and a region of hills to the east rising gradually to over eight thousand feet. The whole country is very fertile as the climate is sub-tropical and it gets plenty of rain for half of the year during the monsoons. In the plains, besides the coconuts which are used for every conceivable purpose, supplying both food and fuel, oil for lamps and thatching for roofs and coir for matting and brushes, etc., there is also an abundance of rice; and in the hills there are large tea and coffee plantations, originally the work of Europeans but now mostly owned by Indians. This makes it one of the richest states in India, but at the same time it is the most thickly populated not only in India but in the world, and this sets a grave economic problem. With this it has the distinction of being the most literate and best educated state in the Indian Union. It is said that there are more graduates per square mile around Tiruvalla than in any other part of the world. It is this combination of wealth and poverty, of a high level of education with much unemployment, which largely account for the growth of communism in Kerala. On the other hand Kerala has the distinction of being the most christian state in India. Christians are said to number about one fourth of the population, and their influence is even more considerable as they are one of the wealthiest communities.

This will give some idea of the complexity of the situation here, but it is made even more complex by the marked divisions which exist among Christians. The Church in Kerala is said to have been founded by St Thomas the Apostle in the year 52. One's first instinct is to dismiss this as a legend like most of the legends of the apostles, but there is apparently more ground for it than one might expect. The legend derives from the apocryphal Acts of St Thomas, which date from the third century. These are certainly not historical, but they indicate that there was a tradition connecting St Thomas with India in the third century, and they have been found to be correct in certain historical details, so that they cannot be dismissed altogether. They are supported at least in regard to the fact that St Thomas visited India by a very strong tradition among the Fathers. St Ephrem the Syrian, St Ambrose, St Jerome, St Gregory of Nazianzus and St Gregory of Tours all mention the apostolate of St Thomas in India as something to be compared with that of St Peter in Rome, St Andrew in Epirus and St John in Ephesus. It is interesting also to an Englishman to know that Alfred the Great sent an embassy to India in the year 883, headed by Sighelm, bishop of Sherborne, to visit the tomb of St Thomas. This tradition among the Fathers is supported by a wealth of local tradition, which cannot, of course, always be trusted, but which nevertheless generally has some historical basis. Local tradition here points to seven churches which are said to have been founded by St Thomas himself. I visited one of them some time ago. It is a modern church and there are no remains apparently of the ancient church, nor have I been able to find any sign of written records in regard to these churches. By the side of the church, however, there lives a family which claims to be directly descended from one of St Thomas's converts and to have lived in that place ever since. This shows something of the tenacity of local tradition which one finds everywhere here.

The most important witness to this tradition is St Ephrem the Syrian. He was a deacon of Edessa in Mesopotamia in the fourth century, and records not only that St Thomas preached the gospel in India but also that he was martyred there and that his bones were afterwards removed to Edessa. This evidence is important, because if anything is certain, it is that the Church in India was from the earliest times closely connected with the east Syrian or Chaldean Church, of which Edessa was one of the principal sees. It was from this church that the Church in India received its liturgy and for many centuries it was subject to its jurisdiction. We may take it for certain then that the Church was established in India in the fourth century and that it was in close touch with the Church of Edessa. There is also an interesting tradition that a certain Thomas of Cana, a Syrian, came to India in the year 345 and settled there with a group of Syrian families. It has been suggested that these people were driven out of Persia by the persecution of the Church there and so found their way to India. In all this it must be remembered that there was regular trade at this time between India and the West, and it is known that there were Jewish colonies in India before the time of Christ, so that there is nothing improbable in such intercourse.

Whatever may have been its origin, then, we may take it for certain that the Syrian Church has existed in India at least from the fourth century. For the next thousand years it continued its existence undisturbed, deriving its orders from the metropolitan of Persia. Unfortunately in the sixth century the metropolitan of Persia followed the greater part of the Syrian Church into schism. There is no evidence throughout this period of intercourse between Indian bishops and the Holy See, but it must be admitted that the history of the Church during this period is obscure.

However when the Portuguese came in the fifteenth century, the Syrian Church was recognized as being both Catholic and Orthodox and enjoyed full communion with the Holy See. But then begins one of the most tragic incidents in the history of the Church. The Portuguese were for the most part unable to conceive of a Catholicism other than the Latin Catholicism which they themselves professed and they began a campaign to force the Syrian Church to accept the jurisdiction of a Latin bishop and to change their rites and customs. This led to a disastrous schism which has continued to the present day. Large sections of the Church broke away from Rome and placed themselves under the jurisdiction of the Jacobite Patriarch of Antioch, while those who remained faithful to Rome were forced to accept a Latin hierarchy and to suffer the mutilation of their ancient rite. It is only within the last thirty years that the Syrian Church has been given its own hierarchy and allowed to develop on its own lines. There is now a movement to restore the liturgy to its original form, but centuries of latinization have done their work and it is difficult now to restore what has been lost.

In the meantime the Syrian Christians who separated from Rome have themselves suffered many divisions. The main body of them was divided until recently into two sections, one directly subject to the Patriarch of Antioch, the other claiming a certain independence under its own *Catholicos*. In addition to this another party broke away in the last century under the influence of the Church Missionary Society and established a Reformed Church known as the Mar Thoma Church, while another group joined the Church of England and now forms part of the Church of South India. When one adds to this the numerous Protestant missions, and other sects, it can be seen how complicated the position is. There is however one encouraging sign. The movement of reunion with the Holy See, started over thirty years ago by Bishop Mar Ivanios, has continued to grow year by year.

There are now over one hundred thousand Jacobites reunited with the Catholic Church. These people use not the
east Syrian rite which was formerly used in Kerala, but a
west Syrian rite derived from Antioch, and when they
return to unity with Rome, they are encouraged to preserve
their rite and customs.

This rite is of great interest. It is one of the oldest rites in
the Church and goes back to the ancient rite of Antioch in
the time of St John Chrysostom. The Syriac language is
closely akin to the Aramaic which was spoken by our Lord
and the apostles, and not unlike Hebrew. The liturgy has
preserved an extremely primitive Hebrew character and one
feels very close to the sources of Christianity. It is richly
dramatic and symbolic and the whole liturgy takes the form
of a dialogue between the priest, the deacon and the people.
It is perhaps the best example of a fully corporate act of
worship which it is possible to find. This is made effective
because for a long time now the liturgy has been celebrated
in the vernacular. Here in Kerala it is said (or rather sung,
for the whole liturgy is chanted and all the people know
the chants) in Malayalam. At present this liturgy is confined to Kerala, but there seems to be no reason why it
should not extend in time to other parts of India and be
said everywhere in the local language. It has the advantage
of being an eastern liturgy, which has already been well
tried in India and obviously has a deep popular appeal.
This, however, is a difficult and controversial question. The
Latin liturgy is now established all over the north of India
and there is already considerable rivalry between the two
rites. It is difficult to say what form the liturgy in India will
finally take. Some have suggested that a specifically Indian
rite might eventually be evolved from the Syriac and Latin
liturgies, but that is looking far ahead. The problem is
serious as it must be admitted that Catholicism has not yet
found its authentic expression in India. The Latin Church

on the whole remains a western European institution and is felt to be foreign to Indian tradition. The Syrian Church is authentically Indian owing to the centuries during which it has been established here, but it is still confined to Kerala.

It is not merely a question of rites and ceremonies, but of a wholly different tradition of life and thought. The eastern Church has preserved a way of life and thought, which finds expression in its liturgy, which is quite different from the tradition of the West. It knows nothing of scholastic philosophy and theology, or of moral theology and casuistry. But it is steeped in the tradition of the bible and the Fathers and the ancient symbolic mode of thought. Unfortunately in our seminaries the training tends to be almost entirely western in character, so that the Syrian Church is in constant danger of being westernized. Only recently the Holy See had to issue an instruction insisting that the eastern customs such as standing and not kneeling during the liturgy and of using ikons and not statues should be preserved. These may seem small matters but they are of vital importance if the eastern tradition of the Syrian Church is to be maintained. If the eastern churches are to be brought back to union with Rome they must be assured that all their traditions and customs shall be preserved, so that the eastern element which is essential to the fullness of Catholicism may not be lost. In the wider perspective of India and the Far East, it may be said with certainty that the only hope of the spread of the gospel in these parts is that it should be presented in an authentically eastern way, and it is the eastern Church with its eastern liturgy which is best adapted to this end, because it preserves a tradition of life and thought and worship, which is both eastern and Catholic. The Catholic Church, wrote Pope Benedict the Fifteenth, in words which should be impressed in the minds of all Catholics, is neither Latin nor Greek nor Slav but universal. Unless the Church can show herself Indian in India and Chinese in China and

Japanese in Japan, she will never reveal her authentically catholic character.

It may be said that here in Kerala there is a kind of crucible in which the Church in India is being tested. Christianity is stronger here than in any other part of India. The Church is represented by both the Latin and the Syrian rites and has an opportunity of developing a Catholicism which is both eastern and Indian which exists in no other part. There is also an opportunity for the work of reunion among Christians which is exceptionally favourable. At the same time the Church is confronted with communism more dramatically here than in any other part of India. Thus all the major forces which are shaping the future are represented here and it remains to be seen what time will bring out of this crucible.

3. Hinduism and Christianity in India

IT IS a remarkable fact that the Church has been established in India for over fifteen hundred years and has had for the most part everything in its favour, and yet in all this time hardly two in a hundred of the people has been converted to the christian faith. The position is, indeed, worse even than this figure would suggest, as the vast majority of Christians are concentrated in a few very small areas and in the greater part of India the mass of the people remains to-day untouched except in a very general way by the christian faith. It is necessary to go even further than this and to say that for the immense majority of the Indian people Christianity still appears as a foreign religion imported from the West and the soul of India remains obstinately attached to its ancient religion. It is not simply a matter of ignorance. This may have been true in the past, but in recent times there has been a remarkable revival of Hinduism, which is more or less consciously opposed to Christianity, and the educated Hindu today regards his religion as definitely superior to Christianity. These facts, which can scarcely be questioned, suggest that there has been something wrong with the way in which the gospel has been presented in India (and the same remark would apply to all the Far East) and especially in the relation which has been established between Christianity and Hinduism.

It is not as though India were in any sense indifferent to religion or opposed to any new form of it. On the contrary, the Indian people may be said to be the most religious people on earth. For five thousand years India has lived on a

continuous tradition of religion. Its beginnings can be traced
back to the time of the beginning of religion in Egypt and
Mesopotamia, but while the religion of Egypt and Babylonia
has become a thing of the past, as dead as Greek religion,
the religion of India has undergone a continuous evolution
and has emerged today as one of the great living faiths of
mankind, so that it even attracts converts from the West. In
the course of this time Hinduism itself has undergone a
remarkable transformation, while yet remaining true to its
inmost 'idea', and at the same time India has given birth to
other forms of religion, like Buddhism, Jainism and Sikhism,
which remain no less vital today than Hinduism itself. Why
is it that Christianity has remained outside this living stream
of religion as a thing apart and has failed to penetrate into
the religious spirit of India? Is it due to the nature of
Christianity itself or is it due to some failure in the christian
apostolate?

Perhaps we can best approach this subject if we consider
the background of the Church in India. The number of
Catholics in Kerala alone is almost equal to that in all the
rest of India, and almost half the vocations to the priesthood
and the religious life in all India come from Kerala. This then
is the first thing to be noted, The Church in India is largely
concentrated in one small area, from which priests and
religious are sent out all over India as 'missionaries'. The
majority of these Catholics belong to the Syrian rite, though
there is also a considerable body of Latin Catholics deriving
from the time of St Francis Xavier and the Portuguese
missions of the sixteenth century. Very little is known of
the history of this Syrian Church from the fifth to the
fifteenth century. It seems to have preserved its faith
and its integrity in its isolated state by becoming what
was practically a separate 'caste' among its Hindu neighbours. Thus the Syrian Church remains wonderfully integrated in its social customs with the surrounding Hinduism.

Christians do not appear here as foreigners, but are a distinct but perfectly integrated element in the social life of the country. In their religion on the other hand, the Syrian Christians seem to have kept rigidly aloof from Hinduism. Until recently they showed no power of expansion whatsoever; they remained a people apart, exercising no apostolate. In recent years a great 'missionary' movement has grown up among them and they send out priests and religious, as has been said, all over India. But their Catholicism is now, apart from the liturgy, entirely western in all its forms of piety and thought and it shows no more capacity to enter into vital contact with Hinduism than any other form of Christianity in India.

The other great concentration of Catholics in India is to be found in Goa and its offshoots in Bombay and Mangalore. This Church derives from the expansion of the Portuguese Empire in the sixteenth century and it is here that the great weakness of the Church in India is to be found. The gospel was brought to India in the train of the Portuguese armies and the policy of the Portuguese was to make their converts renounce all their distinctive Indian customs (which were considered to be tainted with Hinduism) and to become Portuguese as far as possible in every way. They were given Portuguese names (which they retain to this day) and compelled to adopt European habits of food and clothing, which meant that they became 'outcastes' to the Hindus. Not only were all the forms of religion, liturgy, theology and devotional customs of a rigidly western pattern but all the external forms, churches, statues, paintings and music, were faithful copies of western models. It is difficult to exaggerate the effect that this has had on the Church in India. The Goan Catholics are today in a sense the *élite* of the Church in India. They have preserved an extremely firm faith (and in this respect it must be said that the Portuguese policy has been successful) and have a great many vocations to the priesthood and the religious life. After Kerala the majority of 'missionary' vocations in India come from Goa and Mangalore, and what is perhaps even more important, the majority of the bishops in north India come from this Church. But with all their admirable qualities, the Goan Catholics remain cut off from the main stream of Indian culture. It must be said that in the last few years they have begun to awake to this fact and a great effort is now being made to 'adapt' the Church to Indian culture which is having considerable effect. But the consequences of the past cannot be wiped out in a day. It is this more than anything else which has made the Church in India appear as a foreign importation and a relic of colonialism. It is this which has kept the Church isolated from the main stream of Indian life and incapable of penetrating to the heart of the people. Though through the labours of St Francis Xavier and other apostles of his kind the Church was able to win converts in the first century of Portuguese rule, the number of converts, at least among the educated, has since then been negligible.

In regard to this it must be said that the failure of the Church to win converts among educated Hindus corresponds with the failure to win converts from Buddhism or Islam in other parts of the world. We are compelled to ask again whether it is not due to some failure in the method of the apostolate. In fact we find in India, as elsewhere, in general no attempt was made to understand the religion of the people to whom the gospel was to be preached. On the contrary, it was generally treated with the utmost contempt and condemned without consideration as 'paganism' and 'idolatry'. Can we be surprised that Christianity has so often been despised and hated in return? Even a holy man like St Francis Xavier, who is moreover the patron of Catholic missions, made no attempt at discrimination. To him all Hindus, but especially Brahmins, were 'devil-worshippers', the Buddhists were 'atheists', the Moslems were 'infidels'. It may surely be said that an attitude like this makes it morally impossible to win converts, except by a miracle of grace on which only a saint like St Francis could rely. But for the ordinary missionary it has meant that the hearts and minds of educated people are necessarily closed to the gospel.

There have, however, been exceptions to this general rule. In China there is the example of Ricci and his fellow Jesuits who, by studying the Chinese classics and living as mandarins, were able to win a sympathetic hearing among the most learned and religious of the Chinese; and in India there is the wonderful example of de Nobili, who by living as a sannyasi (one who has renounced everything to seek God alone) and making a deep study of the Hindu scriptures was able to win even the Brahmins to his faith. De Nobili, in fact, gives us the key to what was wrong in the christian approach to the Hindu and shows how the gospel might have been presented to India in such a way as to attract its deepest minds and its most religious men. De Nobili worked in the Tamil Nad, that is the region of South India between Kerala and Madras, with its centre at Madura, one of the great 'sacred' cities of India. He found in Madura a Portuguese priest who had been there eleven years without making a single convert. His mission was entirely confined to the poor fishermen, the people to whom St Francis had preached, who were regarded as 'outcastes' by the Hindus. As a *parangi* (a Portuguese, the name which was, significantly, given to all Christians) this priest was himself regarded as an 'outcaste' and his mission was therefore doomed to failure from the start. De Nobili immediately changed all this. He became a sannyasi, that is one who has reached the highest stage of the spiritual life and is considered to be 'above' caste, and scrupulously observed all the rules demanded of this state (such as not eating meat, fish or eggs, or drinking alcohol, and observing perfect poverty, chastity and religious devotion). In this way he immediately found the way open

to him to approach the Brahmins and the other caste Hindus
and to win a hearing for the gospel.

Though de Nobili eventually obtained the approbation
of the Holy See for his method of apostolate, yet the constant
and unscrupulous opposition of the Portuguese to all his
efforts at evangelization made his work almost impossible.
Yet he left behind him a considerable body of converts
from among the Brahmins and the other caste Hindus, and
his apostolate was continued after him by his followers,
Beschi and de Britto. In the nineteenth century, after the
suppression of the Society of Jesus, all this work ceased and
a return was made to the conventional methods of preaching.
Yet in spite of this there remains to this day in the Tamil
Nad a Catholicism which one feels to be more closely integrated with the surrounding culture than in any other part
of India.

In de Nobili's method of evangelization there are two
elements which need to be considered in relation to the
apostolate today. There is first of all his study of the sacred
writings of Hinduism. De Nobili made himself a master both
of Sanskrit and of Tamil, the Tamil language being second
in importance only to Sanskrit in the religious culture of
India, and he seems to have obtained a deep and thorough
knowledge of the Vedanta. In the second place de Nobili
lived as a sannyasi; that is, he adopted the traditional way
of life of a 'holy man' in India. Both these seem to be
essential elements in the apostolate in India and in both
respects he has had followers in modern times. The study of
the Vedanta has been principally the work of the Jesuits in
Ranchi near Calcutta. Two great Sanskrit scholars, Fathers
Dandoy and Johanns, edited for twenty years a periodical
called *The Light of the East*, in which an attempt was made
to relate the Vedanta to Catholic philosophy in a series of
articles called 'To Christ through the Vedanta'. These articles
were by Father Johanns and represent the most thorough

and systematic attempt to study the different schools of the Vedanta in the light of the philosophy of Aquinas which has yet been made. His contention was that all the elements of a perfect system of philosophy, or rather of natural theology, existed in the Vedanta, but that as it lacked the idea of creation, in the proper sense of *'creatio ex nihilo'*, it was never able to establish the true relation between God and the world. Either it had to say with Sankara that the world, as such, has no real being and that God alone is the one reality 'without a second'; or it had to say, with Ramanuja and the other masters of the Vedanta, that the world is in some sense a 'part' of God, a 'mode' of the divine being. But once the doctrine of creation was introduced, he believed that it was possible to construct a perfect system of Christian philosophy on the basis of the Vedanta.

The work of Father Johanns has not yet received the attention which it deserves. His mode of exposition is perhaps too much westernized to appeal to Hindus, though many expressed their appreciation of his learning. On the other hand, Indian Catholics as a whole remained impervious to any serious study of Hindu thought and *The Light of the East* had to cease publication for lack of support. Yet this task of the confrontation of Hindu and Catholic thought remains one of the principal tasks of theology in our time, and the work of Father Johanns and Father Dandoy (whose *Ontology of the Vedanta* was published in French with a commentary by Maritain and Olivier Lacombe in 1932) must be considered the most important pioneer work in this direction. There are happily other Jesuits who are continuing these studies today in India, but there are few Indians among them. Yet it is to Indian Catholics that we must look ultimately for the development of theology along the lines of the Vedanta and the production of what may be called a christian Vedanta which would show how the doctrine of the Vedanta finds its proper fulfilment in Christ.

But perhaps even more important than the study of the Vedanta is the following of the ascetic life, which has always been characteristic of the Hindu seer. For the Hindu, philosphy has never been merely an abstract science but always a way of salvation. It is a 'theology' in the deepest sense, a way to God. The word which is used to describe the state of one who is engaged in the study of the Vedas is *brahmacharya*, which can best be translated as 'seeking God' and which is held necessarily to involve the observance of chastity. Moreover, those who have reached the final stage in the search for God are called 'sannyasis', that is men who have made a total renunciation (*sannyasa*) of the world and live in absolute poverty. It cannot be doubted that if the Church is ever to penetrate deeply into the inner life of Hinduism, it will be necessary to have christian sannyasis who are prepared to live in the same kind of poverty as the Hindu. This involves something much more than the normal standard of religious poverty in the West. What is considered poverty in the West is regarded as luxury by the Hindu. A single full meal of rice and curry a day (without meat, fish or eggs), a mat to sleep on, bare feet or at most sandals for walking; these are considered the norm for a sannyasi and there seems to be no reason why a Christian should not adopt these customs.

The most serious attempt to follow this way of life in modern times is that of Father Monchanin, a French priest of saintly character and remarkable learning, who came out to India in 1940 to work under the Bishop of Trichinopoli in the Tamil Nad, not far from the scene of de Nobili's apostolate. After working for ten years as a poor parish priest in this district, he joined with a French Benedictine monk, Father le Saux, to establish an ashram on the banks of the sacred river Kavery, not far from Trichinopoli. The ashram consisted of small huts of brick with a concrete floor and a thatched roof and no furniture, built in a mango

grove by the banks of the river. They had a small oratory
built in Hindu style, the sanctuary taking the form of a
mulasthanam (the inner shrine of a Hindu temple) and a
narthex for the people being attached in the style of a *manda-*
pam (the outer court of a temple). Here they lived in the
utmost simplicity, wearing the kavi dress of the Hindu
sannyasi, going barefoot, sleeping on a mat on the floor, and
adapting themselves in all their habits of food and behaviour
to Hindu customs. Those who visited them there know how
deep was the silence and solitude, the atmosphere of peace
and of the 'desert', in this ashram.

But there was more than this. Father Monchanin and
Father le Saux were both deep students of Hindu thought,
but they also realized that the ultimate ground of meeting
between the Church and Hinduism must take place not in
the realm of thought but in that of contemplation. Behind
all Hindu philosophy, behind all its search to know God,
there is a still more profound impulse to experience the
reality of God, to participate in the very being of God. This
is the ultimate quest of the soul of India, which has inspired
its religious tradition from the time of the Vedas to the
present day. Unless the Church can answer this desire, unless
she can show not merely that she possesses the true knowledge of God but also that she can lead souls to the experience
of the truth, to that wisdom which passes all understanding,
she will never reach the soul of India. This was the ideal for
which Shantivanam (the 'abode of peace') stood. It was to
establish a school of the contemplative life in India which
would correspond with the most profound aspirations of
the Indian soul, to lead India to the fulfilment of its quest
for the experience of God by showing that it could be found
in Christ.

Unfortunately this initiative in the contemplative life met
with practically no response. Indian Catholicism appears to
be still too deeply rooted in its fear of Hinduism (a fear

based on ignorance) to be able to make this contact with
the Hindu tradition at its deepest level. When Father Monchanin died rather suddenly in 1957, Father le Saux was left
alone and externally nothing had been achieved. Yet it is
difficult to believe that his work has failed. We must rather
believe that he was a pioneer, the fruit of whose labours
have yet to be seen. Like Charles de Foucauld, perhaps, he
was ahead of his time and we may hope that the seed which
he planted will one day bear fruit.

The ideal of a contemplative life adapted to India is, however, still being continued at Kurisumala ashram. The
co-founder of this community, Father Francis Mahieu, is a
Cistercian of the abbey of Scourmont in Belgium. He came
out to India in 1955 in search of the contemplative life in an
Indian form and lived for a year at Shantivanam. But he
was then led to start a new foundation in Kerala on somewhat different lines. Kerala, as has been said, is the strongest
centre of Catholic life in India. He felt that if the contemplative life was to take root in India, it must first be planted
here in the very heart of the Church. The life of this ashram
is, therefore, based on the Syrian liturgy, a liturgy which is
extremely rich in biblical imagery; it is in fact an offshoot
of the semitic genius and as it were a continuation of the
poetic genius of the Semites in christian times. The life is,
therefore, deeply rooted in the soil of the bible and of
biblical tradition. At the same time, an attempt has been
made to return to the sources of monastic tradition, to the
Fathers of the Desert, not only to Cassian and the Egyptian
fathers but also to the great Fathers of the Syrian tradition.
Thus, though based on the Rule of St Benedict with a strict
Cistercian observance, the life may be said to have a definitely
eastern character. As yet no attempt has been made to link
up with the Hindu tradition except in externals. It is felt that
the Indian Church is not yet ripe for a meeting with Hinduism at a deeper level.

Yet it may be hoped that if the contemplative life can thus be established within the Church in a form which is attractive to Catholics, it may eventually provide a meeting place, in which contact can be made with the Hindu mystical tradition. The Church has first of all to recover her own foundations, to return to the sources of the monastic life, to the bible, to the primitive liturgy, to the 'holy fathers' to whom St Benedict referred his monks for the daily inspiration of their lives. Only when the contemplative life has taken root and begun to grow in this way may we hope for that contact with the living sources of Hindu spirituality by which the Church may ultimately be enriched. But always this must be the goal. India must find the answer to her own quest for God in Christ and she must find it her own way. It must come as the fulfilment of her own tradition, the end to which by secret ways God has been leading her from the beginning of her history.

PART TWO

Towards an Indian Catholicism

4. *The Incarnation and the East*

TO BELIEVE in the incarnation is to believe not merely that
God became man, but that God became man at a certain
time and in a certain place. It is to believe that the divine
has entered human history and given it a new meaning and
a new direction. It was no accident that Christ was born in
Judaea, when Herod was king, and Augustus was emperor.
He came in his own words when 'the time had been fulfilled',
at the moment which St Paul was to call the 'fulfilment of
history'. The whole history of the world had been leading
up to this point and the whole of history since that time is
determined by it. For the incarnation does not affect man as
an individual alone; it affects the whole of human culture
and civilization.

This can be seen in the first great crisis in Christianity,
which is reflected in the New Testament. Up till this time
the divine revelation had been confined to the Jews. The
Jewish culture had remained a thing rigidly apart, stren-
uously fighting for its own tradition and refusing all but the
minimum contact with the Greek and Roman world. With
the coming of Christ this barrier was broken down; 'He
made of the two nations (Jew and Gentile) one,' as St Paul
said, 'breaking down the wall that was between them.' Thus
with Christianity the Hebrew tradition entered into the inheritance of the Graeco-Roman world, and it is to the
fertilizing contact of these two cultures that the Church
owes her liturgy and theology and canon law.

The next great crisis in the history of the Church was that
of the barbarian invasions of the fifth and sixth centuries.

Having assimilated the culture of Greece and Rome, the Church was faced with the hosts of 'barbarians', Goths, Lombards, Franks, Saxons, living outside the borders of the Roman Empire. Again it was the fusion of these two cultures, the Graeco-Roman culture of the Church and the primitive but strong and deep culture of the barbarians, which produced the civilization of the Middle Ages.

Thus the incarnation set in motion a development of history by which the Roman Empire became christian and then, with the conversion of the barbarians, first of the western nations and then of the eastern Slavs, the whole of Europe. The incarnation, we may say, was extended to the whole of Europe; for the Church is nothing else, in Bossuet's words, than Jesus Christ extended to mankind.

The next phase in this development of history came with the Renaissance and the discovery of America. Another continent was added to the sphere of the incarnation. At the same time there was the beginning of missionary endeavour, with St Francis Xavier, in the Far East. It is true that there had been Christians in India from an early time and that there were nestorian Christians in China in the seventh and eighth centuries, but one cannot speak of a real cultural contact of Christianity with China and India at this time. But can we speak of any real cultural fusion of Christianity with the people of the Far East even at the present time? It is a remarkable fact that in spite of christian missions over a period of four centuries, Christianity has still only touched the fringe of the civilization of the Far East.

What is the reason for this? It is surely the fact that Christianity has been presented to these people in a form of western culture. It has never penetrated the inner life and thought of the East. Thus it is left for us at the present day to face the next great crisis in the history of Christianity, the extension of the incarnation to the East. Christ has become incarnate in Europe and America; He has still to become incarnate in Asia and Africa. Africa, however, does not present such a serious problem; for the native cultures in Africa are not sufficiently strong to demand any great modification of the form in which Christianity is presented to them. But the civilizations of China and India are not only of the greatest antiquity but also culturally the most profound which the Church has encountered since the first days of her mission in the Roman Empire.

It is a remarkable fact, as Karl Jaspers has pointed out in *The Origin and Goal of History,* that in the sixth century before Christ a movement of thought took place which was to shape the destiny of the greater part of mankind for all future time. It was the time of the Hebrew prophets in Palestine and the first Greek philosophers in Europe, of Gautama Buddha and the seers of the Upanishads in India, of Lao-Tzu and Confucius in China. Each of these movements seems to have risen spontaneously without contact with the others and each developed along its own lines so as to form a separate culture. At a certain point, as we have said, the Greek and the Hebrew traditions met and blended, and in the same way with the spread of Buddhism in China and Japan, the Indian and Chinese traditions were fused. But until the present day there has been no comparable fusion of the eastern and the western traditions.

This, then, would seem to be the problem with which we are faced today. We realize, as never before, that we belong to 'one world'. Politically and economically, no one nation can stand apart from the rest. At the same time during the last fifty years the wisdom of the East has become known to us, as it had never been known before. A book like Aldous Huxley's *Perennial Philosophy,* with its very extensive bibliography, shows how far the fusion of eastern and western thought has already gone on a more or less popular

level. Mr Huxley's conception of the relation between
eastern and western thought, like that of René Guénon,
Coomaraswamy, and other exponents of eastern tradition,
is, of course, not satisfactory from a christian point of view,
but it puts the problem before us in all its urgency.

We are faced with a tradition of philosophy and mysticism,
of art and morality, of a richness and depth not excelled,
and perhaps not equalled, by the tradition of Greek culture
which the Church encountered in the Roman Empire. What
then is our attitude towards it to be? It is clear that we cannot simply reject it. The attempt to impose an alien culture
on the East has proved a failure. There are no doubt elements
in this tradition which we may have to reject, just as the
Church had to reject certain elements in the Greek tradition.
But what is required of us is something much more difficult.
It is an effort of discrimination, such as the Greek Fathers
from Clement and Origen to Gregory of Nyssa and Dionysius the Areopagite undertook, not merely rejecting what is
wrong but assimilating all that is true in a vital act of creative
thought.

It was by this creative energy that the structure of theology
was built up by the Greek Fathers, gradually assimilating
the principles of platonic philosophy until they had been incorporated into the very tissue of christian thought and
life. In the same way we know how St Thomas and St
Bonaventure in the Middle Ages took up the thought of
Aristotle and built that also into the structure of Catholic
theology. It is also important to remember how very great
was the influence of the Arabian philosophers, Avicenna
and Averroes, on the mind of St Thomas, so that a vital
contact was made at this point between the christian and
the islamic traditions.

We have, therefore, in christian history the evidence of a
continuous movement of assimilation, by means of which

different forms of culture have been integrated into the christian tradition, to guide us in our attitude to the cultures of the East. This process of assimilation may extend not only to modes of thought but also to forms of worship. The best example of this is the development of the slavonic liturgy in the ninth century with St Cyril and St Methodius. It is possible that we may see a corresponding development in China. We know that permission for a Chinese rite was granted in the seventeenth century, though it was afterwards unfortunately withdrawn; and Abbot Lou, the great Chinese convert, who became a monk of St André in Belgium, was of the opinion that China would never be wholly converted to Catholicism until a Chinese rite was again permitted. What is certain is that there will have to be a contact between Chinese and christian thought on a deep level, before the Chinese mind will ever become christian. Abbot Lou suggested the foundation of a Chinese college in Rome, at which both the Chinese could study Catholic theology and Catholics, in turn, could become acquainted with the Chinese classics.

The same process is obviously required in our approach to India. There is need for a profound study of the doctrine of the Upanishads and of the whole tradition of the Vedanta, and also of Buddhist thought of both the Hinayana and the Mahayana schools. This is a work which will require the greatest discretion. We cannot afford to reject any of our western heritage, as it took shape in the thought of Aquinas, but at the same time we have to open our minds to what will be a genuine development of thomism, bringing out vast potentialities which are latent in it. There is already much that is common to the western tradition based on Plato and Aristotle and the eastern tradition both of China and India. What is required is a meeting of the two traditions at a deep level of understanding, so that their full potentialities can be realized. This will require on our part

a real effort to assimilate the mode of eastern thought, for
eastern thought differs from our own most of all in its mode.
Whereas western thought tends to be rational and discursive, eastern thought is intuitive and contemplative. The
one is the product of the *animus* the other of the *anima*. The
difference is therefore primarily psychological.

The meeting of the eastern and the western minds will
thus be a true marriage of East and West, the masculine
mind of the West meeting with the feminine mind of the
East in a fertile union. But if the union is to be really fruit-
ful, it will require a generous giving of self on either part.
For a long time now the West has taken the path of extro-
version. We have concentrated on science and mechanics
and all forms of rational philosophy. We stand in desperate
need of the opposite process of introversion, of intuitive
thought and interior life such as the East can teach us. On
the other hand, the East is now turning to our western
civilization, whether in its communist or its capitalist form,
and is in danger of losing its own roots in tradition. The
meeting of East and West which we have in mind, therefore,
will be a return of both to what is deepest in their own
traditions, the recovery of their roots in the past.

The advantage which we ourselves may hope to gain from
this is immense. There are already a great number of people
in the West who owe their conversion to Christianity to the
discovery of eastern thought. It would seem that the superficial manner in which the christian faith is often presented
has driven many people away from the Church, and it has
required the contact with the mind of the East to make
them realize the deeper aspect of Christianity.

For those who already possess the faith, the deepening
of their life of prayer and the enlargement of their insight
into the mysteries of the faith can be considerable. But if
eastern thought is to have this effect upon us, we have to

approach it with great reverence. We must realize that the tradition of the East embodies what is practically a revelation of God to mankind. It is derived from that primitive revelation of God in the order of nature, which was made to man in the beginning, and was renewed in the covenant with Noah. For Noah is the Father not only of the Jews but also of the Gentiles; he is a type with Melchisedech and Job, of that primitive religion which existed all over the world before the election of the Jews and the special revelation made to them. Though this primitive revelation has been obscured and distorted in some respects, it remains nevertheless at the basis of the eastern tradition.

We have, therefore, not merely to impose a western religion on the people of the East, but to show them that their religion finds its true fulfilment in Christ. Clement of Alexandria maintained that what the law was to the Jews, philosophy was to the Greeks – a 'pedagogue' to lead them to Christ. We may say the same of the great philosophical traditions of India and China. The Buddha, Confucius and Lao Tzu were genuine precursors, as Guardini has said, preparing the mind of the East for the coming of Christ. It is through them that the people of the East have up till this time received the light and grace of Christ.

This then is the new light of the incarnation for which we have to look at the present day. Christ has to become incarnate in the East, not as a western teacher come to destroy what they have learned from tradition, but as he came to the Jews, as the fulfilment of all their hopes and desires. Doubtless this will present the same test for the East as it presented to the Jews. There will be the temptation to cling to the old forms and refuse to allow them to grow into the new life which Christ brings. But there must be nothing done on our part, as far as we are able, to alienate Christ from them. We have to remember that Christ belongs neither to the West nor to the East. By divine providence he was born between East and West, and belonged to a people which could mediate between the two. Our religion is not western in its essence, nor is it eastern. It transcends the division of East and West, and offers the one ground on which the two can be united.

Once again we recall the words of Pope Benedict XV: 'The Catholic Church is neither Latin nor Greek nor Slav, but universal.' There has been a Latin and a Greek and a Slav Catholicism, all differing profoundly in their forms of worship and their mode of thought, and yet essentially one in their faith and communion in the one body of Christ. There is no reason why there should not be a Chinese and an Indian and perhaps also an African Catholicism differing no less profoundly, and yet no less essentially one. For Christ must become incarnate among all men, revealing himself to each people as the fulfilment of its own deepest aspiration and at the same time bringing it into the unity of the whole body of mankind. For in the words of Père de Lubac, 'Christ is the "form" which humanity must put on in order that it may truly be itself.'

5. Fulfilment for the East

INDIA TODAY is going through a critical phase in its history. Its people have become independent again, and India is engaged in establishing its position as a world power. It has taken over the forms of our western civilization, and the process of transformation into a modern democratic state is under way. Industrialization is going ahead rapidly, and in a great city like Bombay one finds all the latest developments in modern style and technique. Everywhere one sees magnificent buildings, banks, insurance companies, technical institutes, hospitals, cinemas, huge blocks of flats in concrete, and palatial mansions in a blend of all the styles of East and West. There are electric trains, buses (curiously reminiscent of London) and taxis everywhere, and the most luxurious American cars. But with all this the old life of the East goes on relatively undisturbed. The bazaars in the heart of the city are as picturesque and colourful as ever; men go about barefoot and clothed in all manner of costumes; the women in their *saris* walk with a grace and dignity which puts modern fashions to shame; and children swarm everywhere, running about barelegged and carefree. The total result is an astonishing fusion of ancient and modern, of East and West, and yet somehow harmonious and coherent.

Here is a whole new world which is coming into being, rich with promise for the future of mankind. For it is not only the future of India which is at stake. India has taken all that the West has to give, both good and bad. With our political institutions and our economic techniques, it has taken also our western habits of life and thought.

Everywhere one sees American films and American maga-
zines, and in the bookshops are all the latest products of
western science and philosophy. Inevitably, India is being in-
fected by the materialism and scepticism of the West, whether
it comes in the extreme form of Marxism or the more enlightened forms of western humanism. The question is
whether or not the spiritual tradition of India can withstand
the shock of western materialism. On this point, it is not too
much to say, the fate of the world depends. It is not the
conflict between communism and the West which is really
fundamental, but the conflict between materialism in all its
forms and the spiritual tradition of mankind, of which India
is a great representative.

Throughout its history, India has been devoted above
almost all peoples to the search for God. Indian religion
has been called the 'most searching quest for the divine in
the natural order that the world has known.' The characteristic of this religion is that it has always ranked contemplation
and the contemplative life as the supreme goal of human
life. Some of the earliest Indian scriptures were the work of
men who retired into the forest to live lives of solitude in
meditation and asceticism. To this day it remains the ideal of
Hindu religion that after passing through the two first stages
of life, that of the student and the householder, a man should
pass on to the higher stage of renunciation of the world and
contemplation in preparation for death. A similar ideal of
contemplation as the end of life was held among the ancient
Greeks, but for the Greek, contemplation always tended to
centre on the nature of man and the universe. In India, on
the other hand, contemplation has always been concerned
not with man or nature, but with the ultimate reality, the
true Self, which is the ground of all existence.

We in the West have inherited the tradition of the Greeks,
and our attention, especially since the Renaissance, has been

concentrated on the study of man and the universe. As a result, we have built up a body of scientific and humanist knowledge which has transformed the world, but we have almost entirely lost the knowledge of God, of the ultimate reality without which all other knowledge can only lead to disaster. That is the tragedy of the West, and it has led to the threat of physical destruction which faces us today. If we are to recover our sanity and save our souls, we have to discover again the true source of knowledge, of life and reality, and learn to integrate our science and humanism with this perennial truth.

What is the nature of the spiritual tradition which is found in its purest form in India and constitutes the supreme heritage of mankind? It is simply this. There is one absolute, eternal, infinite, unchanging Being, which is the unique source of all existence, of all knowledge and of all life; which is above all things and in all things and for which all things exist. This absolute Being may be conceived in different terms, but in one form or another it is the basis of all religion, not only in India but in China and throughout the East. This is the basis of what we have called the spiritual tradition of mankind and the ground of all religion.

What, then, is the relation of man and the universe to this absolute Being? Man is an image of God; the universe is a finite reflection of this infinite Being, a reflection of the One in the many, of the eternal in time, of the infinite in space. Here again this relationship may be differently conceived, but fundamentally it will be found that this is its nature. The universe is not an 'illusion' as it is sometimes said; it has a certain reality, but it is the reality of a reflection in a mirror. Apart from its source it has no reality at all. The real illusion is to mistake the material universe for an independent reality. This is the great illusion of the West, which constitutes materialism. It is against this illusion that the whole of eastern doctrine stands, by affirming the absolute reality of

God alone and the wholly dependent and relative reality of
the physical universe.

How does man enter into relation with this infinite and
eternal Being? Here again there is a deep cleavage between
East and West. We in the West have grown up under the
influence of Aristotle and the Greeks. We think of reason
acting upon the evidence of the senses as the normal mode
of human knowledge. But in the East it has always been
understood that there is a higher mode of knowledge than
sense or reason – the knowledge of spiritual intuition, a
knowledge not dependent on the senses or on any logical
process, but on the soul's direct, intuitive awareness of itself.
It is this which has been sought in the East from time im-
memorial and which gives the true knowledge of God. It is
a knowledge derived from contemplation, a wisdom which
descends from above and directly enlightens the soul. To
this knowledge all images and concepts can only act as
'supports'; it transcends the finite order and unites man
directly with God.

This, we would say, is the basis of all oriental doctrine,
of that spiritual tradition which underlies all ancient religion
and which survives today in India and the East. But granting
this, there are two questions which have to be asked. First,
what is the validity of this claim to a higher mode of
knowledge? And, secondly, what relation does the whole
of this tradition bear to Christianity, and particularly to
Catholicism?

We have to recognize that this tradition is not found only
in the East. It entered into the current of western thought
with Pythagoras and Plato and finds its most eminent ex-
ponent in the West in Plotinus. Such a concourse of the
greatest minds of East and West, covering thousands of
years of human history and permeating the religion of
millions of people, is surely in itself an impressive witness

to its truth. In a sense, of course, it cannot be proved. One can only prove it by experience, just as if someone claims that a play of Shakespeare or a symphony of Beethoven gives him a unique kind of experience, one cannot either prove or disprove the validity of the claim. It is a matter of experience.

But for a Catholic there is evidence of another kind. The influence of Aristotle, with his logical and analytical method, on our philosophy and theology has been so great that we sometimes forget that our theology was originally formed in the school of Plato. The Greek Fathers were almost all Platonists, and the founder of Latin theology in the West, Augustine, has left on record the fact that he owed the first illumination of his mind to Plato. It is, in fact, precisely this spiritual tradition of the East, coming to us through Plato and Plotinus, which lies at the heart of our Catholic theology. When Aquinas introduced the exact method of Aristotle into theology, he did not discard this platonic tradition; on the contrary, he incorporated it. His theology is a synthesis of Plato and Aristotle based on the original Hebrew-christian revelation.

St Thomas' conception of God is identical with that of eastern tradition, as we have described it. In the question of the relation between the universe and God, St Thomas introduced an exact conception of creation which clarifies the eastern tradition, but leaves it essentially unchanged. And in the matter of the knowledge of God by contemplation, St Thomas clearly recognizes a mode of knowledge above both reason and faith, admitting man to knowledge of God by experience, an infused wisdom in which the soul becomes passive to the divine action, *patiens divina*.

We have, then, the right to say that this spiritual tradition is an integral part of Catholicism. It is, in fact, nothing but that perennial philosophy, that universal metaphysical tradition, which is the basis of all religion, both eastern and

western. To this tradition Catholicism gives a precision
which is generally lacking in the East. It firmly upholds the
absolute transcendence of God, while admitting his imma-
nence in all creation. It asserts the reality of the material
creation while allowing that this reality is wholly relative
and dependent on the absolute being of God. Above all, it
brings the whole of this tradition into relation with the
doctrine of the incarnation, of man's salvation through the
redeeming death of Christ and his need of God's grace if he
is to enter into a living relation with him.

Catholicism thus acts to confirm and strengthen the tradition of the East by giving it its centre in history and making
it a dynamic force in the world. It is here, surely, that the
hope of the future lies. If we could recognize the profound
affinity which underlies the religions of East and West and
explore more and more deeply this metaphysical doctrine
which we hold in common, we should open the way to an
approach to the East on a deeper level than has yet been
made. Then we should perhaps be able to lead the East to
see that their own tradition is wonderfully fulfilled in
Catholicism, losing nothing of its richness, but receiving
strength and confirmation. At the same time we should find
our own faith enriched and enlarged.

For this is not simply a matter of philosophy. We cannot
enter into the eastern tradition unless we are prepared to
meet its representatives on the level of contemplation. It is
in union with God – beyond images and concepts – in the
ground of the soul that the true meeting must take place.
This means that we have to recover our own contemplative
tradition, to penetrate more deeply into the mystery of the
scriptures and the liturgy, to follow out consistently that
path of purgation, illumination and union, which leads to
an experimental knowledge of God. In other words, we have
to revive the contemplative life among ourselves.

It is a remarkable fact that until recently there has not been a single contemplative monastery for men in India. The Church in India has grown wonderfully in recent years: from being a missionary Church a with largely foreign clergy, it has grown into a great national Church with its own cardinal and a large majority of Indian bishops and clergy. It has its schools and colleges and seminaries where Indian priests are being trained; religious orders like the Jesuits, the Redemptorists, the Carmelites and the Franciscans are firmly established. But there are as yet no contemplative monasteries, apart from the heroic attempt, already mentioned, on the part of Père le Saux and the Abbé Monchanin to introduce a strict form of the eremitical life, and a foundation from St André in Belgium, which follows the normal Benedictine tradition of the West, though they have attempted to introduce certain adaptations to Indian manners and customs in the matter of food and clothing. There is surely a great need for a foundation following the traditional pattern of the monastic life, centred on the sacred liturgy and giving contemplation its place as the supreme object of life.

The civilization of Europe was built on these foundations in the Middle Ages. We owe it to the Rule of St Benedict that this ideal of contemplation was kept steadily before men's eyes and all human activity was seen to be subordinate to this one supreme end. If the Church is to fulfil in the modern world her function of keeping before men's eyes the ideal of contemplation as the end of human life, upon which the value and efficacy of all human action and all human knowledge depend, then it is to the contemplative orders that she must turn. In the monastic life, both work and study have their place. A monastery must strive to be self-supporting; it will aim at having its own farm and garden, at producing all that is necessary for its daily needs, at doing all necessary work for itself. But all this work will be kept strictly subordinate to the one object of contemplation and the love of God. All work will be a 'work of God', done in God's service and made as far as possible into a means of union with God. This witness to the essential dignity of labour is surely one of the most important forms of the apostolate in modern times.

In the same way a monastery will have its regular course of studies. These will be based on the scriptures and the Fathers and will aim especially at recovering that deep sense of the 'mystery' of the scriptures, which is our great inheritance from the early Church. But it will not neglect the study of philosophy and theology in that great tradition which found its supreme expression in the *Summa* of Aquinas. It is here that in India there should be found a place for the study of the metaphysical tradition of the East. But this will not be merely a scholarly study of eastern doctrine; like everything else, study must be subordinated to the end of contemplation. We must learn to see in both philosophy and theology not an end but a means towards a deeper apprehension of the reality of God. It is here in particular that eastern thought can help us to realize that all discursive and analytical thought is no more than a mode of preparation for that deeper understanding, that wisdom which comes from contemplation and is the gift of God.

So finally all monastic life will find its centre in the liturgy, the work of God *par excellence*. At regular hours throughout the day and night the monk turns to this act of prayer and worship by which he bears witness continually to the supreme reality of God. This is the function of the monk in the Church, to bear witness by his prayer and his praise and his worship, by the total sacrifice of his life, that God alone is the unique source of life and truth and love in the world. By this means it will surely be possible to unite ourselves with the heart of India, with that spiritual tradition which runs through all Indian life and thought. Then it may be

that India will come to see in the Church the fulfilment of
her age-long quest for God, and in Christ to recognize the
saviour, who alone can deliver us from the power of this
world, from those forces of materialism and scepticism
which threaten to destroy the world.

6. The Missionary Today

IT HAS been a great misfortune that in the past two or three centuries the christian missionary has been identified with the colonial expansion of Europe. Even when he did not come in the train of advancing armies, he owed his position to the influence of his country and he came as the representative of a foreign power. Even so great a missionary as St Francis Xavier never ceased to rely on the power of the Portuguese government, however much he might have cause to regret it, and established his missions in India with its support. The result is that Christianity today is inevitably regarded in the East as an imported religion and as part of that colonial system which the people of the East are bent on eliminating by every means in their power.

It can, then, hardly be a matter of surprise if the Church in India appears to many as a foreign religion, without any vital relation to India's own aspirations and ideals. But fortunately there have been other influences at work, above all the great enterprise of Robert de Nobili, who attempted to introduce an exactly opposite method of evangelization. He lived, dressed and ate as a sannyasi and made a deep study of Sanskrit and of Hindu philosophy, identifying himself in every possible way with Indian life and culture. But unfortunately, de Nobili's experiment was short-lived owing to the opposition which it raised. But he succeeded nevertheless in sowing a seed which is of incalculable importance for the future of the Church in India.

There can be no question as to which method the missionary of today must follow. There is no place for colonialism in any form in the East today. A missionary must come, not as the representative of a foreign power, but as a simple minister of the gospel, to serve the needs of the people and to work in a humble spirit of brotherhood for the welfare of the country. His position is not unlike that of the ordinary Englishman in India today. Since the English left India and ceased to be its rulers, they have been welcomed back as private individuals, who are prepared to serve and not to rule. It is said that there have never been so many Englishmen in India as there are at the present day and that they have never met with so much friendship.

This is surely a lesson for the missionary. If he is prepared to give up all connection with foreign powers and to become an Indian among the Indians, working simply for the good of the Indian people, he may be sure of winning their respect and friendship. India is proud of her tradition of tolerance in religion and is anxious to preserve it in the new democratic order of today. As Pandit Nehru himself said, 'We should always remember that the minority religious communities in India such as Muslims, Christians, Sikhs, Parsees, Buddhists, Jains, Jews are as much part of India as anyone else. . . . So far as religious freedom to propagate one's faith is concerned, every religion has that freedom in India.' If the government has at times restricted the entrance of missionaries into the country, one may believe that this action is due to the fear of introducing too many foreign elements into the country and not to any hostility to Christianity as such.

The situation in India is, therefore, not unfavourable to the spread of Christianity, yet offers serious problems. Christianity cannot claim any privileged status in India. It has to take its place among the other minority religions, and it can rely on nothing but the intrinsic truth of its message. Now this situation involves a definite responsibility towards these other forms of religion. It is no longer possible

for the christian missionary to dismiss these other religious
traditions as simply false religions, as has been done in the
past. The more he knows of these religious traditions, the
more he recognizes how much truth is contained in them,
and a christian apologetic must be capable not merely of
showing the 'errors' in other religions but of reconciling the
various aspects of truth found in them to the universal truth
of Christianity.

Thus, for the christian missionary today, the first require-
ment is to have an adequate knowledge of the religion of
the people among whom he is living. He will never get a
hearing for his own faith unless he is prepared to respect
and understand the faith of others. It is noticeable that in
recent times there have been practically no conversions from
any of the other major religions to Christianity. It is well
known that it is the rarest thing for a Muslim to be converted
to Christianity, but this is also true to a large extent of the
educated Buddhist or Hindu. These people feel that they
have religious traditions of the greatest antiquity which have
bound their peoples together for centuries and have moulded
the character of the race. They cannot be expected to abandon
this inheritance for another religion which, in their eyes, is
no more than a parallel form of religion in the West, unless
they are convinced that it is capable of preserving all those
values in their own religion to which they are rightly attached.

It would seem therefore that an altogether new approach
to the missionary problem is required. We can no longer
hope simply to take Christianity as it stands and impose it
upon other people. Christianity is a religion which itself has
had a long history. It began as the religion of a small group
of people in the Middle East, with a Jewish background and
certain affinities with Greek culture. It grew up in the
Graeco-Roman world, retaining its basically eastern character while being moulded more and more by the influence

of Greek thought and Roman law. From the time of the barbaric invasions in the fifth century, it began to receive the great multitude of Germanic nations into its fold, and as the eastern Church began to separate from Rome, the Church in the West developed along more and more definitely western lines. Since the Reformation, the peculiarly Latin character of Catholicism has been still more clearly emphasized, and the Church, while remaining universal in its essence, has developed that specifically Latin and western form of expression, in its liturgy and theology, its piety and discipline, which is still the mark of Catholicism at the present day.

This markedly Latin character of Catholicism raises its own problems in Europe and America, but when it comes to introducing Catholicism to the East, the problem is accentuated a hundredfold. The whole mould of thought of Latin Catholicism is alien to the people of the East. The great Chinese convert, Abbot Lou, maintained that China would never become christian (even apart from the external pressure of communism) until the Chinese people were allowed to worship with a Chinese liturgy and Latin theology brought into vital relation with classical Chinese philosophy. In India the problem is even more acute. The Church remains cut off by all its habits of thought from those deep sources of spiritual life and thought which have moulded the character of the Indian people for four thousand years. Unless some means is found of making contact with these sources, there seems to be absolutely no hope (except by a miracle of grace which we have no right to expect) of Christianity making any deep impression on the mind of India.

And yet the problem does not admit of any easy solution. We cannot simply discard the tradition of the past centuries in the Church and attempt to return to some primitive form

of biblical Christianity. This would be simply to repeat the
error of the Reformation. The Church is a living organism
which has grown up through the centuries under the continuous guidance of the Holy Spirit. Nothing in its development is sheer chance. It is impossible, even if it were desir-
able, to return to the past. We have to accept the Church as
she is, with all those characteristics which time and change
have impressed on her features. Christianity is not an idea
which can be divested of its earthly garments and clothed
afresh in another dress. The Church is a concrete reality, an
earthly tabernacle which bears within it the living presence
of Christ, and it is only within this living tabernacle, with
all its human defects, that the message of the gospel is preserved in its integrity and communicated to men.

But if we must loyally accept the Church in her earthly,
human nature, we are not bound to limit ourselves to those
particular features which she may wear at the present time.
Apart from all accidents of time the Church continually preserves within herself the whole truth which was communicated to man in Christ, and is capable of drawing at all times
on the depths of the Spirit which resides in her. Already in
Europe and America we are witnessing a great renewal of
the life of the Church. In liturgy and theology, in social
doctrine and in its sense of universal mission, we can see
signs of new life, of an adjustment to the needs of the time
and to the responsibilities which the situation of the world
demands. It is in this spirit that we can hope to find an
answer to the problem of the missionary. There must be
complete loyalty to the tradition of the past and, at the same
time, a readiness to adapt and change, to make experiments
and advance along new lines; in other words, to participate
in the actual growth of the living Church, as the organism
through which the Holy Spirit is working out his purpose
for mankind.

We must remember in the first place that the Church is

by no means bound to the Latin language or to a Latin mould of thought. There was once a Greek and a Slavonic Catholicism as orthodox as any Latin Catholicism. There was an Egyptian Church, a Syrian Church, an Armenian Church, each with its strong national characteristics and yet all equally Catholic. We have to be prepared, on this analogy, for a Chinese and a Japanese Catholicism, an Indian and an African Church, all differing in their modes of thought and expression but all united in the one communion of the Catholic Church. Nor is this merely a matter of language and of external rites. It concerns much more the intrinsic modes of thought and feeling which are characteristic of different races and correspond with what is deepest in their psychology.

This in turn involves a new approach to the whole problem of religion. The study of comparative religions has made it clear that there is no form of religion which does not contain some elements of truth. God has not left himself without witness throughout the course of history. There is a continuous tradition coming down from that primitive revelation which was given to man in the beginning, which is preserved in one way or other in every authentic form of religion. In some cases this tradition has been obscured and corrupted until it is hardly discernible; in others it has been preserved with remarkable purity. If we confine our attention to the principal religions of today, we can say without hesitation that in Hinduism, Buddhism and Islam this primitive tradition has been developed with a wonderful insight, and in its purest forms, as expressed by their great doctors and mystics, it comes astonishingly close to Christianity.

We must realize that we are not dealing here with 'false' religions; we are dealing with a true religion, which has been distorted in certain respects and lost its integrity, but which nevertheless remains an authentic witness to the

eternal truth. Christ did not come to destroy these religions;
he came to correct, complete and fulfil them.

It can even be asserted that these other religions are a
providential preparation for Christianity, by which the people
of the East have been led through the course of their history
towards their fulfilment in Christ. Thus Buddha can be
viewed as a 'forerunner' of Christ; Krishna as a 'type' of
Christ, and even Mohammed as not so much a 'false prophet'
as one who recovered the truth of primitive revelation for
the pagan people of Arabia, and whose message likewise
awaits its fulfilment in Christ.

In our dealings with these religions we must try to discover how, throughout their history, God has been leading
them step by step towards the final revelation of himself in
Christ. We have to show how Christ is, as it were, 'hidden'
at the heart of Hinduism, of Buddhism, of Islam, and how it
is the one Word of God which has enlightened mankind
from the beginning of history and manifested himself to
all the different nations according to their different psycholo-
gies, permitting many errors to remain but never withdraw-
ing the guidance of his Spirit.

The Church thus shows itself catholic by embracing all
truth wherever it is to be found, and by answering to the
deepest needs of all people. But at the same time this encounter with other forms of religion should lead to an
enrichment of Catholic doctrine. The Church possesses all
truth in principle, but it is only gradually, through the course
of centuries, that she is able to give adequate expression to it.
The study of Hindu, Buddhist and islamic thought offers
an incomparable field for the development of Catholic doctrine. There are many today who have found that their
understanding of their own faith has been marvellously enriched by the study of eastern thought. May it not be that
there are certain aspects of the gospel which can only be
brought to light through contact with the eastern mind,

just as certain aspects have been made known through the genius of the Greek, the Russian and the Germanic minds?

All this requires, of course, great humility on our part, a readiness to put away our own preconceptions and to learn from others, to submit to the discipline of other modes of thought than our own and to allow our minds to take the mould of another tradition. But it also requires great faith, a constancy in our own faith and a complete confidence in Christ as the one truth in whom all truth is contained, who is alone able to reconcile the conflicts of religion, and to lead all men into the unity of truth.

7. Catholicism and the East

WHEN WE ask ourselves the reason for the comparative failure of the Church to take root in the Far East and to penetrate its culture, we are inclined to put it down to the association of the Church during the past centuries with the European colonial powers. There is no doubt that this has been an immense obstacle to the spread of the gospel and that it has branded the Church as an alien institution in the eyes of most people in the East. But I believe that there is a deeper reason than this, though it is one which it is very difficult for most people in the West to realize. This is the extremely western character of modern Latin Catholicism even at its best.

The Catholicism which was brought to India and the Far East in the sixteenth century was the Catholicism of the Counter-Reformation. Now there is no doubt that the Counter-Reformation was a very great work in its way. It saved the Church in Europe. But it was an adaptation of the faith to meet a peculiarly European situation, and it marked perhaps the furthest development of the Church in a westerly direction. Its whole mode of thought and action, as embodied in its system of theology and its canon law, was something utterly alien to the eastern mind. There was also the habit of thinking of the christian life in terms of warfare and of the Church as a 'militant' organization. The work of the missionary was often considered as a form of 'conquest' analogous to that of the colonial powers; even now one hears of the 'missionary conquest of the world'. All this inevitably tends to identify the Church in the mind of the

East with western powers and western institutions, and to make missionary enterprise appear as a form of 'spiritual aggression'.

In this perspective very little consideration was given to the temperament, the character or the religion of the people to whom the gospel was to be preached. The faith was considered as a rigid system of doctrine and discipline which was to be imposed on all alike. The religion of the Hindu, the Buddhist, the Moslem, the Confucian, was simply an obstacle to be destroyed. But the culture of the people of the Far East, as also of the Near East, was until recently entirely religious in its character. This meant that the Church was from the beginning excluded from all that was most significant in the culture of these people. Can we wonder that it remained an alien institution and never became assimilated to the life of the people?

It would be foolish to pretend that this mentality has now disappeared. The Church is still to a large extent governed by the habits of mind of the Counter-Reformation. But there is no doubt that a profound change is taking place. Perhaps this can best be seen in the place which the liturgy is now coming to hold in the mind of the Church. We no longer think of the gospel as a system of doctrine which has to be imposed on people indiscriminately, but rather as life which has to be lived, and the liturgy as the expression of this life. It is, in fact, in the liturgy that the Church enters most deeply into the life of a people, takes root in a country and begins an authentic growth. And if it is to do this effectively it has to be adapted to the life and customs and habits and traditions of the people. The spread of the gospel in this light will appear no longer as a form of warfare or of 'conquest', but rather as it is described in the gospel itself – as a kind of leaven. It is not something which is imposed from above, but something which works within the given environment and gradually transforms it. Or it can be

compared, again in the words of Christ himself, to salt in the
earth, an element which mixes with the other elements and
gives them their special savour.

It is obvious that this view of the gospel calls for a completely different approach towards the culture of the East,
and still more towards its religion. It has been described by
a missionary in India recently as a process of 'mutual assimilation'. It is not a question of 'adaptation', in an external and
superficial way; the Church has to enter into the cultural
inheritance of the people of the East as deeply as she once
entered into the cultural inheritance of Greece and Rome
and the peoples of Europe. The language and literature, the
music and architecture, the art and philosophy and religion,
all that belongs to the cultural tradition of a people must
enter into the life of the Church and into the liturgy, which
is the expression of that life. As long as we continue to
worship in 'Gothic' and 'Baroque' churches with marble
altars and statues imported from Europe, we can hardly expect our religion to appear as anything but an alien and
exotic thing in the East. The fact that these importations
are generally in the worst of taste only makes matters worse.

Yet there is a serious difficulty which arises here and perhaps accounts more than anything else for the slowness of
this process of adaptation to the East. Throughout the
orient, whether we are thinking of the Near East or the
Far East, we can say that religion has from the beginning
given its 'form' to the national culture. In India the prevail-
ing culture is Hindu; in Burma and Ceylon it is Buddhist;
in Egypt, Syria and Persia it is Islamic; in China and Japan,
though other elements enter in, Buddhism has had a profound influence. In these great cultural traditions religion
affects every aspect of life and thought and art. It is only
natural, therefore, that there should be a tendency among
Christians to reject the whole cultural tradition along with

its religion. But this only shows the urgent need for a new approach to these religious traditions. There is still a tendency to regard them as 'false religions' and to treat them with fear and suspicion. The ignorance of the average Catholic in India of the spiritual tradition of Hinduism is profound, and I have no doubt that it is so with Buddhism and Islam elsewhere. At best these traditions are regarded as forms of 'natural religion' and as of mere cultural value.

This concept of natural religion, if by that we mean a religion developed by means of natural reason from the evidence of the senses, seems to be entirely misleading when applied to the religious traditions of the East. The very basis of all these traditions is what Rudolf Otto called the 'idea of the Holy', that is the idea of a sacred 'mystery', of a transcendent Being, which is yet immanent in the whole creation and manifests itself to man not so much to his reason as to an intuitive wisdom transcending both word and thought. According to every tradition this Being is not known by reason but by revelation, which is embodied in tradition. It is surely not difficult for us to connect this with our own traditional doctrine that there is a universal revelation of God, which was made in the beginning to all men, and which though often degraded is never entirely lost. Thus there is nothing to prevent our holding that there is an element of genuine supernatural revelation in all the great religious traditions, which has often been jealously guarded, and to see in them not so much false religions as true preparations for the coming of Christ.

God has not left the people of the East outside the sphere of his providence. He has made himself known, though in different measure, to all men. Father Daniélou, in his book *Holy Pagans of the Old Testament*, has shown how the bible itself is a witness to this tradition of a universal revelation made to man before the mosaic or the christian dispensation, and Newman in a remarkable passage of the *History of*

the Arians has spoken of it as the 'Dispensation of Paganism'.
'It would seem, then,' he says, 'that there is something true
and divinely revealed in all religion over the earth, over-
clouded as it may be at times and even stifled by the im-
pieties which the corrupt will and understanding of man
have incorporated with it . . . so that revelation properly
speaking is a universal not a local gift; and the distinction
between the state of the Israelites formerly and Christians
now, and that of the heathen is not that we can and they
cannot attain to eternal blessedness, but that the Church of
God ever has had and the rest of mankind never has had
authoritative documents and appointed channels of communication with him. The Word and the sacraments are
the characteristics of the elect people of God but all men
have more or less the guidance of tradition in addition to
those internal notions of right and wrong which the Spirit
has put into them.'

It is necessary for us, therefore, to approach the people of
these different religious traditions not as our enemies but as
our friends, who share in part the truth which we are called
to preach. At the present time in particular, when the majority of young men all over the world are turning from
their traditional religion towards atheism and scepticism, we
should surely recognize the value of these traditions. What is
needed is some kind of ecumenical movement among the
world religions comparable to that which already exists
among Christians. If we are now beginning to approach our
separated fellow-Christians as our brothers and not as our
enemies, it is surely time that we began to approach our
fellow-men in other religious traditions in the same way.

In the light of this approach we should no longer regard
the elements of religious tradition in the culture of a people
as obstacles to their assimilation. It is well known that the
great Benedictine monk, Dom Odo Casel, held that the early

christian liturgy owed much to the influence of the 'mystery' religions of the Roman world. Whatever the extent of this debt may have been, it cannot be doubted that our liturgy grew up in the climate of this religious world and that it is profoundly affected by it. In the same way we should not be afraid of the influence of the religious world of Hinduism, Buddhism and Islam on our christian liturgy. We have, of course, to guard against syncretism of any kind, but this only means that we have to learn to discriminate within each tradition between that which belongs to the universal religious tradition of mankind and that which belongs to its own limited and particular point of view.

In Hinduism, for instance, to confine our attention to India, there is a most profound sense of 'mystery' and 'sacrament'. No people on earth has gone further towards the penetration of that ultimate mystery which lies beyond all human words and thoughts, transcending every name and form, and yet manifesting itself in all the forms of nature and of human consciousness. Here we have perhaps the deepest expression which can be found of the primeval revelation of the presence of God in nature. The Hindu temple is itself essentially a 'sacrament', a representation of the divine mystery manifested in nature and the human soul. On the outer walls will be depicted the world of nature, of plants and animals and men gradually rising to the world of the gods. As we approach the inner shrine, we are led through various degrees of purification, until we reach the holy place, the garbha griha, which is the 'centre' at once of the universe and of the soul. It is the 'womb' from which all things spring and at the same time the 'cave within the heart', the secret place where man enters into communion with the ultimate mystery. If it is a temple of Siva there will generally be a lingam in this inner shrine. This has caused much feeling of horror and disgust among Europeans, especially Christians, but properly understood there is nothing 'obscene' about it.

It represents on the one hand the 'source of life' and on the other hand the absolute 'formless' divinity, the stone barely shaped in contrast with the wealth of imagery elsewhere.

This is but one example among many of the depth of meaning which underlies Hindu art and religion. We shall also find in Hinduism ideas of trinity, of incarnation, of salvation and grace, of sacrifice and sacrament. All of these may be considered as part of the inheritance of the primordial tradition, which have their counterpart in the other religious traditions. There are, of course, profound differences to be found among these different religious conceptions and one of our principal tasks is to discriminate between them. The christian idea of trinity and incarnation, for instance, is profoundly different from the Hindu and we must never confuse them. But it is just this work of discrimination which is required of us, seeking to discover what is common to the two traditions and where the essential difference lies. It is not a question therefore of refuting the 'errors' of Hinduism or any other religion, but of discrimination and discernment in a spirit of sympathy and understanding.

In this way the Church may be able to enter into the full tradition of Hindu culture, as of Buddhist and Islamic, drawing from them all those elements in the religious tradition of the East which can be incorporated into her own life. At the same time these traditions will profit by their contact with the living truth of Christ. They will learn to discover Christ as the true fulfilment of all these ideas which are contained within them and which only receive their full meaning when they are understood in relation to Christ. The trinity, the incarnation, grace and redemption, sacrifice and sacrament, all these ideas are properly revealed only in Christ. Rama, Krishna, Siva and the Buddha, all the mysteries and sacraments of Buddhism and Hinduism, are types and shadows of the mystery of Christ.

Thus if the Church is to enter into the cultural inheritance of the East, she must enter into the heart of its religious tradition, 'saving' everything which is good and true and purifying everything which is erroneous or corrupt. This may well be the work of centuries, involving a task as complicated as that by which the Church built up dogma and liturgy in Europe, through intercourse with the world of Greece and Rome and then of the Germanic peoples.

Yet, it may be asked, where are we to start? I would say that we have first of all to recover the sense of mystery and sacrament in our own liturgy. We must try to see our faith as our forefathers saw it, not as a system of rational and moral concepts, but as a divine mystery, an economy of grace totally transcending the reach of reason. It is in this way that we can make contact with Hinduism at its deepest level, and perhaps learn from it a deeper sense of our own christian mystery. In the second place we have to recover our sense of symbolism; to understand how the liturgy is throughout a symbolic representation of the mystery of Christ. A symbol in this sense is a sign which in some way makes present the thing which is signified. It is in the liturgy above all that the mystery of the presence of God, of which the Hindu is so keenly aware, should be made manifest. If the Hindu could learn to see in the christian Church the true temple of God, where the living God dwells among his people and makes them one body with himself; if he could be brought to realize the wonder and the mystery of the sacramental presence, by which we are able to touch and taste God as he himself has sought to do throughout his history, would not the Church then be a living witness to the mystery of Christ which would touch the eastern soul? Finally, this means for us a return to the sources of our faith, to that eastern tradition of Hebrew and semitic thought, which lies behind all the later development of

Greek and Latin theology. We have to learn to draw once again on all the riches of symbolic theology contained in the bible. All this treasury of eastern wisdom lies hidden within our western liturgy, especially in its use of the psalms, but if we are to recover the full force of this Hebrew tradition, I am inclined to think that we shall have to turn to the eastern liturgies, especially to the Syrian, which preserves more than any other the spirit and the form of the original Hebrew and which already has taken deep root in India.

Our Latin liturgy, though it has its own peculiar beauty, remains characteristically Roman and western, not only in its language but also in its spirit and structure, in its music and gestures. I must confess that when I first came out to India I thought that the Latin liturgy had an absolutely universal character and that one had only to take it, with its plainchant in the Benedictine tradition, in order to bring home to the Indian people the mystery of Christ. But I have come now to doubt whether this is so. The Latin liturgy has a sobriety and restraint and an air of almost military precision which is foreign to the eastern soul. The genuflection, for instance, was, I believe, originally the gesture of the Roman soldier before the emperor; but when an oriental enters the divine presence, he prostrates on both knees with his forehead touching the ground, and this is what we do in our Syrian liturgy. Again in the Roman mass the priest at prayer is instructed to hold his hands at the level of his shoulders and to extend them with palms facing inwards, but when an oriental raises his hands in prayer he will hold them widely extended with the palms turned upwards and this again is the custom in the Syrian rite.

These are small things, but they are deeply significant. The gestures of the body express the ingrained habits of the soul, and it is in these things that the radical differences between human beings become most conspicuous. I must mention one other example. In the East when anyone enters a holy place, whether it is a temple, a mosque or a church, he invariably removes his shoes (like Moses in the presence of the burning bush). But when one of our Indian priests approaches the altar, he is instructed to put on shoes and socks. In that simple fact is a measure of the gulf which still separates the Church from the people of the East.

8. Christ and India

It is a matter of no little interest that Christmas should be a public holiday in India. It means that Christmas takes its place among those Hindu and Moslem festivals which mark the course of the year in India and are occasions for general rejoicing. It might be said that this means that it is accepted only as a social festival (as it is in so many places in the West now), but I think that it is more than that. There can be no doubt that Christ has entered now into the pattern of religious belief in India. One has only to think of the place which he occupied in the life and thought of Mahatma Gandhi. But, significantly, he is not the Christ of Easter – I have often found Hindus completely ignorant of the very idea of the resurrection – but the Christ of the Sermon on the Mount. Christ is for them a great teacher, like the Krishna of the Bhagavad Gita, (and it is worth remarking that it is just those aspects of his teaching which are almost ignored in the West that make the deepest appeal to the Indian mind, like the saying, 'Resist not him that is evil').

But many a Hindu would go further than this and see in Christ an *avatara* like Krishna, that is a manifestation of God. Of course, this has a very different meaning in the Hindu mind from the christian doctrine of the incarnation. A Hindu believes that God is continually manifesting himself throughout the course of history. In a sense all the 'gods' are to him but manifestations of the one supreme Being, the 'one without a second', who alone supremely 'is'. But he believes also that God has manifested himself from time to time in certain holy men, of whom Rama and Krishna are

the great examples, and to these he is quite willing to add
both Mohammed and Christ.

A perfect example of this is Ramakrishna, the great saint
of modern Hinduism, to whom it owes more than to any
other man, and who is himself regarded by many as an
incarnation. He was a Hindu of the Hindus, brought up in
the purest tradition of Hinduism, but later in his life he
deliberately set himself to 'become' a Christian and a Moslem, that is to meditate on Christ and Mohammed as *avataras*
and so embrace, as he thought, both Christianity and Islam
in his religion. This is enough to show the difficulty of
preaching the christian faith in India. It is always in danger
of simply being absorbed in Hinduism, just as in the early
centuries Christ was in danger of becoming one of the gods
of the Roman Empire.

This comes out in many ways in the daily life of the people.
Hindus will have no hesitation in joining in a christian
religious festival. They will take part in the processions,
singing hymns and listening to the prayers. They will often
indeed be found to pray most devoutly to our Lady and
the saints, and wherever there is a famous shrine, especially
where cures are known to take place, the Hindus will be as
numerous as the Christians. The matter is further complicated by the fact that the Christians often tend to adopt
Hindu customs and ways of doing things. I once joined in
a Catholic procession at a church in Bangalore, where the
statues of the saints were carried in procession, and I could
not help seeing that it was almost exactly like a Hindu procession, where the statues of the saints had taken the place
of the 'idols' of the gods. Yet I think that it is generally
recognized that the christian processions are more reverent
and prayerful than the Hindu and less like a holiday in the
modern sense.

In Kerala the relations between Christians and Hindus

are extraordinarily interesting. There are towns and villages
where the Catholics number 90 or even 98 per cent; it is
almost like living in Italy or Ireland. But this extraordinarily
solid strength of the Church has been built up over the
centuries because the Christians formed themselves into
what is practically a separate caste. (Even today when a
schoolboy fills in an entrance form for a school he puts
down 'Caste – Christian'.) In the early days this was probably
the only way in which the Christians could preserve their
identity and not be submerged in the sea of surrounding
Hinduism. But it meant that the Christians observed the
most rigid rules of caste. There are many Christians living
today who remember how in their childhood a person of
low caste was not allowed to come within so many yards of
the house, and they treated an 'untouchable' exactly as the
Hindus did. As the Christians themselves formed one of the
higher castes, this gave them considerable power and influence. It is necessary to bear all this in mind when one
considers the position in Kerala today, where the communists are exploiting the grievances, both of the past and
present, of the lower castes.

Thus in their social customs the Christians in Kerala have
practically identified themselves with the Hindus. The result
is that Kerala is one of the few parts of India in which one
can say that the Christians really belong and in which the
Church appears as something authentically Indian. On the
other hand, by keeping themselves a separate caste they have
been able to preserve their faith in extraordinary purity.
One feels here, as I have said, that one is living in Italy or
Ireland. The faith has the same kind of solid, traditional
character. On the other hand it must be admitted that it
often has the weakness of a traditional faith. There is evidence
on all sides that the young people, especially at the universities, are not being given an understanding of their faith on
a level with the rest of their education, and as a result many

are being attracted to communism. The Church appears reactionary, especially in the social field, and the communists are regarded as the only 'progressive' and practical people.

Yet one does catch a glimpse here of what a really Indian Catholicism might be. On the great religious festivals in some of the towns the streets will be hung with coloured streamers and huge processions will wind through the streets as the people sing hymns and songs and recite the rosary, all in the native Malayalam. At Christmas every house will have an illuminated star hung over it, and carol singers will go around and find a welcome in Hindu no less than in christian homes.

In the Syro-Malankara rite the Christmas liturgy is of especial interest. It begins at one or two o'clock in the morning with the equivalent of Matins and Lauds, which are sung in the vernacular. (It is characteristic of this rite that on every Sunday before the Qurbana, that is the mass, the office of Sapro, which is the equivalent of Prime, is sung in the vernacular, all the people taking part in the singing of the psalms which they know by heart.) There is then a ceremony of the fire, rather like the lighting of the holy fire in the Easter Vigil in the Latin rite, which takes place at the porch of the church, all the people going in procession round the fire singing the hymn of the angels. Then follows Sapro (Prime) and finally the Qurbana, the whole service taking about five hours.

It is nothing unusual for a service to take several hours. The ordinary service on Sunday will often take three hours or more. People come to church to spend the morning there and no one is in a hurry to leave. I have often been with the bishop on a visit to a village church on a Sunday morning. All the people come out to meet him. Bunting is hung out, fireworks explode (an invariable feature of any celebration here), and a procession with gorgeous silk umbrellas of red and green and purple and orange is formed to escort the

bishop; songs and hymns are sung in Malayalam and sometimes there is dancing. The people feel that it is their day
and their service and they have come there to enjoy it.
Sometimes after the service there will even be a meal taken
together, a kind of agape, all the people sitting on the ground
and eating from banana leaves.

There is no doubt that the sense of religion is still extremely strong in India. Millions of people go on pilgrimage
every year to the sacred shrines – Hindu, Moslem and
christian – on their great festivals. The temples and churches
are thronged with worshippers and they are happy to spend
hours in prayer and worship. I shall never forget the visit
I paid to a Hindu temple to witness the famous Malabar
dance called Kathakali. The ceremonies began at six o'clock
in the evening with *puja* (worship) in the temple and continued throughout the night until six o'clock in the morning.
All the precincts of the temple were filled with people from
the surrounding villages who had come to spend the night
there.

The dance was the most wonderful thing of its kind I
have ever witnessed. It was essentially a sacred dance, representing the stories of the gods and heroes of the Hindu
epics and was acted in a strange hieratic way. The actors
wore elaborate masks which were painted in a traditional
manner and the gestures were strictly formal. There were
no words at all but the whole drama, which was often in-
tensely exciting, was enacted by means of most wonderfully
subtle and expressive gestures. It was accompanied by a
weird music on some very simple instruments (drums and
triangle and a pipe).

The effect of all this, the gathering in the open air under
the moon, the dark faces crowded together watching the
spectacle, the lights in the temple shining out and the strange
unearthly music of the pipe and drums was one of extra-

ordinary 'sacredness'. One felt what it might have been like to have been present at a Greek play in Athens in the time of Aeschylus. There was a sense that the 'gods' were present; it was their mysteries which were being enacted and for the time being one was in another world.

It is this sense of the 'sacred', the 'holy', which gives its strength to religion in India. Everywhere there are sacred places, sacred hills, sacred streams, sacred trees. Indeed there is hardly an outstanding hill or river or tree which has not got its shrine. A peasant working in a field will often build a little shrine in clay and offer his worship there, and on every bus, at least in the country, there will be a little picture of one of the gods or goddesses with flowers placed before it. In Kerala, there will often be a picture of the sacred heart or of our Lady instead, and everywhere along the road one finds crosses and shrines erected. Thus religion still underlies the whole life of the people, and Hinduism and Christianity are strangely interwoven in the fabric of Indian life.

Yet it must be admitted that religion, and especially Hinduism, is going through a critical period now. The young people, especially in the cities, tend to throw off religion entirely. Few of the students at the universities go to the temple now, and christian students tend to be affected in the same way. But it is here that the strength of Christianity may begin to show itself. It is the weakness of Hinduism that with all its depth of religious feeling and philosophical insight it is inextricably bound up with mythology. Indeed it would be true, I think, to say that Hinduism is based on mythology. The gods are symbols of the divine mystery, many of them profoundly significant, but they have no reality in themselves. Even Rama and Krishna, upon whom, above all, Hindu devotion rests, are not properly historical figures. They are epic heroes who have become deified by the religious

imagination of India. However beautiful and significant
these figures may be, it is inevitable that, as modern education spreads, their reality is more and more questioned. The
university student is beginning to lose his faith in them.

But one must not exaggerate. 1 knew a group of university
students at Bangalore, one a very close friend, and I was
astonished at the deep roots which this ancient mythology
had in their minds. The roots are in their blood and in their
ancestry; they are continually fostered at home by the custom
of prayer and the influence of the family, especially the
women, and by regular visits to the temple. And these roots
often seem strong enough to withstand a modern education.
My friend was a good example of this. He was studying for
a degree in commerce and was extremely modern and western in most of his ideas. During the week he dressed in shirt
and trousers like any young student at a university. But on
Saturday, if I went to the little temple of the god Hanuman,
which is quite close to our monastery, I would find him
officiating in the temple, dressed in nothing but a *dhoti*, that
is a plain piece of cloth wound round the middle, and with
his Brahmin cord across his breast. He might have been an
Egyptian priest officiating in a temple in the year 3000 B.C.

In India one continually encounters this paradox of a
primeval religion surviving in the same person beside the
most up-to-date ideas and customs. Yet there is no doubt
that this has set up a conflict in the mind of the Indian today,
a conflict which may become critical within the next generation. With all its depth of religious instinct, its sense of the
sacred, its fervour of devotion, its ascetic and mystical tradition and its philosophy, which reaches the highest level ever
attained by human thought, Hinduism remains bound up
with a vast system of mythology which a modern mind
must find impossible to accept. It is here, surely, that we
must look for the true place of Christ in India.

As long as he is regarded as a symbolic figure like Rama

and Krishna, Christ can never have a true birth in the Indian soul. But when it comes to be realized that he is in reality a historical figure, that he suffered under Pontius Pilate, was crucified, died and was buried, that he is the point at which God enters history, not as a symbol but as a person, to change the course of history and to transform it, then the decisive point in the history of India may also be reached. For Christ alone is capable of reconciling the ancient tradition of religion in India with the demands of the modern mind. He is the fulfilment of all that the imagination of the Indian soul sought to find in its gods and heroes, in its temples and sacrifices. But he is also a human being, who enters into history, who remains in his Church as a living power capable of transforming its economic and political and social life. His story is, if one may say so, the myth become true. The resurrection of Christ is at once a historical fact, which has changed the course of history, and also a symbol of that ultimate truth in which human life and history can alone find their true meaning.

When the Hindu mind comes to recognize the mystery of Easter, the fact of the resurrection, which sets Christ apart from all *avataras*, when it acknowledges the uniqueness of the incarnation, only then will Christmas find its proper place in the life of India. Then one may hope also that all the genius of India, its depth of religious insight, which has never been equalled in history, may find its true centre in Christ and build up in India a Church which will surpass all others in the depth of its understanding of the riches of Christ.

PART THREE

Towards a Non-violent Society

9. The People of India

IT IS difficult for a European, and I would think still more so for an American, to form any real idea of the poverty of India. Even after ten years' stay in India I still find it difficult to take the full measure of it.

One can perhaps begin to form some idea of the standard of living by saying that the average wage of a farm labourer or unskilled worker in the country is a little more than two rupees a day, or about three shillings. This is considered a living wage for a man and his family. The corresponding wage of seventy rupees a month (about five pounds) is the normal wage of a low-ranking post office official, policeman, soldier or school teacher. This may be called a minimum living wage, which rises to ninety and one hundred and twenty rupees as you ascend the scale. A doctor or a professional man of any sort may get two or three hundred rupees or more, but he is far above the level of the ordinary man.

How do people manage to live on five pounds a month? One must consider first of all their houses. The ordinary villager lives in a little cottage of mud walls, which are baked hard in the sun and become almost like brick, and a thatched roof. The floor is of earth, which is painted with a solution of cow dung as a disinfectant and is very clean and pleasant. Many of these cottages are not more than six by six by six feet and have no windows or lighting of any sort, except what comes through the door.

In this single room the cooking is done and the family sleeps and eats. Except for a few pots, either of brass, which

are kept beautifully polished, or of plain earthenware, there
is no furniture at all. It is a universal custom, even among
those who can afford something else, to eat and sleep on
the floor. Beds are common among those who are a little
better off, but tables and chairs are still the luxuries of those
who strive to imitate the West. There is generally no sanitation at all.

The ordinary man lives on rice and curry, and if he has
one good meal a day this is considered sufficient. But many
cannot afford rice, which is often expensive, and they live on
some substitute. In Kerala it is tapioca, a root not unlike a
potato and of about the same food value. In Mysore it is
ragi, a grain which grows very easily and is very sustaining.
In addition there are vegetables and fruits, though their food
value is often not very great, and some people have a little
meat or fish. Milk is very scarce, and butter and cheese are
unknown, except in the form of *ghee*, which is taken with
rice and curry. There are millions of cows in India, but the
average cow does not yield more than about three pints of
milk a day. Eggs are very rarely seen.

In regard to clothing, a man wears a *dhoti*, a piece of cloth
wound around the waist and going down to the feet, and a
woman wears a sari, a single piece of cloth covering both
the upper and the lower part of the body. Most men now
have a shirt, which they wear when they want to dress up,
but at home they prefer to go naked to the waist. I have
found that even doctors and people of some position will
discard their shirts when they want to relax at home. Until
recently it was customary even for women to go naked to
the waist in many parts, but this has altogether ceased now.
It may be mentioned that these clothes are always kept
beautifully clean, and the shirts, which are generally worn
hanging down outside, even over trousers, have a certain
style which gives an air of distinction.

In fact, though what I have described may be thought to represent the poorest level of existence that it is possible to find, it would be a great mistake to think that it is lacking in beauty and dignity. The Indian villager lives very close to nature. Going barefoot and bareheaded (against both sun and rain he wears a towel which is wrapped round his head like a turban and put on and off at need) and frequently, as I have said, bare to the waist, his body has a beautiful natural poise and dignity. The men in Kerala are strikingly handsome; their skin is of a rich bronze colour, and though they are generally slight in build their bodies are graceful and well made. It is only when one lives in a country like this that one begins to realize the beauty of the human body and to understand what it must have been like to live in fifth-century Athens, so much so that I have often wondered that Kerala has not produced a school of sculptors.

The women have a quiet, grave kind of beauty and their saris are often in the most strikingly beautiful colours. They have the custom also of carrying waterpots on their heads, which gives their carriage a superb dignity. One of the commonest sights is to see the women gathered round the well, with their brass waterpots all shining brightly and their bright coloured saris, reminding one of a scene from the Old Testament.

It can be seen from this that though the Indian village may be poor, it is nevertheless full of beauty. One must remember, too, that the villager lives most of his life in the open. His house is for protection from the rain and for cooking and sleeping, but his life is lived in the open under the sun. All this beauty – the palm trees and the fertile fields of rice and large shady trees by streams of water – makes one think of paradise. There is certainly a serpent in this paradise, but it still has something which has been practically lost in the modern world.

In addition to this external beauty, there is also a deep

interior beauty in an Indian village, which few people suspect. The Indian family is one of the most beautiful things in the world. An Indian village is made up of families which are held together in the closest bonds of affection. Unfortunately, the caste system is still very strong in the villages, and one still finds everywhere groups of *harijans* – children of God, as Mahatma Gandhi called them – the 'untouchables', who live apart from the rest and cannot even share the same well, and the division between other castes may be equally rigorous. But within the close circle of the caste there is an immense warmth of affection. Every child in a village belongs to a family group which surrounds him with this warmth, and this continues throughout his life. Even if he goes away for a long time, the village still remains his home and he is sure of a place there.

This warmth of affection is shown particularly towards children. An Indian village may seem very poor and derelict, but it will always be cheered by the sight of children playing. Here again everything is supremely natural. Little children go quite naked, and their elders wear only a cloth around the waist. Children are loved by everybody and grow up in an atmosphere of security and happiness. The older ones look after the little ones; nothing is commoner than to see a young boy or girl carrying a little brother or sister on the hip – children are always carried on the hip and not in the arms as with us.

Despite all this affection and attention, children do not seem to be spoiled. Perhaps there is too much natural hardship in the life to make this possible, but I think it is more the result of moral discipline. Parents are feared as well as loved, and there is a traditional hierarchy in the family which has to be respected.

This moral discipline is especially evident in the relation between the sexes. Boys and girls after childhood never mix in Indian society; this is true even in the towns, though customs are changing. Even in Bombay I noticed that one saw separate groups of young men and of girls going about, but never mixed groups. According to Indian customs boys and girls live separately even at home. The women often take their meals together after the men. In church the men and women always stand in different places, and they are kept apart in buses and railway carriages.

This has had the effect of preserving a remarkable moral purity in Indian family life. Marriages are arranged by the family and the young couple rarely see each other before marriage. Again customs are changing, but it is remarkable how strong this custom remains. It may have disadvantages from a modern point of view, but it undoubtedly leads to stability in marriage which we in the West may envy. My impression is that the Indian family is more stable, more moral and more affectionate than the ordinary family in the West.

All this leads to a deep psychological security in the Indian character, at least in the villages where the traditional customs prevail. This is something of incalculable importance which we have to set against their extreme poverty. In the West we have raised the standard of living immeasurably, but we have lost that contact with nature and that psychological stability and security which the Indian villager still retains.

There are many people who want to remove the poverty at all costs and never stop to think of the price which may be paid. Yet if modern 'civilization' is allowed to break up the stable background of Indian society, as it has done so often elsewhere, it may well be a curse rather than a blessing. For we must remember that with this stable family background there goes in India a deep religious sense. Everywhere among Hindus, Moslems and Christians one finds a deep sense of the religious order of life. I have scarcely ever met an Indian in the country who was without this deep natural piety and sense of divine providence in his life. It is this which enables him to endure the poverty and privation of his daily life with dignity and cheerfulness and above all with unwavering patience. These are virtues which no people can afford to sacrifice.

Yet none can question the need for change; even if anyone were inclined to do so, the change has, in fact, already begun. The old order is changing even in the Indian village and a new world is coming into being. The question is not whether change must take place, but what direction the change must take. We must remember that even at best the Indian villager gets barely enough to eat at present, and if a bad harvest comes, or sickness or any other misfortune, he is immediately brought to the verge of starvation. The life expectancy of a man in India is only thirty-two years, and one child in every four dies before he is one year old. This is the situation which the government of India has to face, and it is trying by every means in its power to raise the standard of living in the villages.

The first great need of the Indian farmer is water. In most parts of the country there is only a season of two or three months' rain in the year; for the rest of the year the farmer must remain idle unless he can find some means of supplying water. The government has introduced several large irrigation schemes, which are very costly and will take time to produce any results, but they will eventually make a vast difference.

Of more immediate value is the digging of wells and tanks in the villages. These form one of the elements in the community projects, which are being extended all over India and aim at enabling the villagers to help themselves. These projects aim further at providing better seed and stock and improved methods of agriculture. At present the Indian farmer makes use of a plough, which is simply a forked

stick, drawn by two oxen, which only scratches the surface
of the soil. It is amazing to discover how even the simplest
tools and implements are still almost unknown. A wheel-
barrow, for instance, is scarcely ever seen. When a mass of
earth has to be removed, it will be carried by women in
little baskets on their heads. Loads are always carried on
the head – even the porter at the station carries your boxes
on his head – and when a road is being built, the concrete
will be carried (usually by women) in small loads on the
head. In the same way there are no carts or other implements
for harvesting. The corn is cut not with a scythe or sickle,
but with a little knife (again usually by women), and the
threshing is often done by treading out the grain with the
feet or by letting the oxen tread it out.

Yet it would be a mistake to suppose that the remedy is
to be found in the introduction of modern machinery. It is
generally agreed that the use of tractors would simply cause
unemployment on a vast scale and disrupt the whole economy
of the village. It is rather at the introduction of improved
methods which are in keeping with the village economy
that the government is aiming. In this it is following out
the ideas of Mahatma Gandhi.

Gandhi, it will be remembered, believed that the salvation
of India was to be found in her villages. For this reason he
made the spinning wheel the symbol of all his work. He
wanted to introduce spinning into every village so that the
villager would be able to clothe himself and to support himself when agricultural work was impossible. He had no faith
in industrialism and the centralized bureaucratic state which
goes with it. He wanted the villages to become independent
and self-supporting and to learn to govern themselves.

Mahatma Gandhi's ideas have been taken up by his
disciple Vinoba Bhave (pronounced Barway), with the full
support of the government and of the other political parties,

even the communists. Vinoba became famous in 1951 when
he entered the state of Hyderabad, which was then practically
under the control of the communists, and started his movement of Bhoodan, or land-gift. In opposition to the communists he conceived the idea of asking the landlords to
give up some of their land to the landless, instead of taking
it from them. The result was beyond all expectations. Very
soon hundreds of thousands of acres were being donated,
and up till now the figure has reached five million.

This is far below Vinoba's goal, for he wants fifty million
acres to solve the land problem of India, but it is a significant
beginning. He obtained this result by walking from village
to village all over India, talking to the villagers and discovering their real needs. He himself is an ascetic, a holy
man, such as India has always revered. He gets up every
day for prayer at three in the morning, then sets off on his
walk (until recently it was twelve to fifteen miles a day) and
then settles in one of the villages for the day to interview
the villagers. He eats next to nothing, living mainly on
curds, as he has a stomach ulcer. It is characteristic of Vinoba
that he calls this his 'blessing', because it has enabled him to
reduce his food to the minimum necessary for life.

From the day when as a young man he first met Gandhi,
Vinoba has dedicated his life to the service of God, but like
Gandhi he has learned that the service of God is to be found
in the service of one's neighbour. Perhaps the most characteristic story told of him is that one day when he had spent the
whole day interviewing two thousand villagers, in the evening, when he was asked whether he was not feeling tired, he
answered simply, 'I have been visited by God over two
thousand times today.'

What is Vinoba's plan? He aims like Mahatma Gandhi
at restoring the Indian village to its original independence.
Now that the first phase of the Bhoodan movement is over
and a large amount of land has been given, the emphasis of

the movement is rather on *grandan*, that is, the 'village gift'. Whole villages have been offered to him and he seeks to organize them on co-operative lines. The land belongs to the village as a whole and the villagers co-operate in its cultivation. The distribution of the land is made according to the size of families, the amount of land they previously held and other considerations, and thus is capable of a great deal of variation, but the point is that the distribution is always made by the villagers themselves. In effect, they form a kind of independent republic and learn to manage their affairs for themselves.

Vinoba undoubtedly believes that land, like air and water, should be held in common. He regards all alike as the gift of God. If it is objected that this is simply 'communism', I think that it can be fairly replied that it is christian communism. It should be remembered that many of the Fathers (notably St Ambrose and St John Chrysostom) held that all land was originally a common gift of God, and only sin has introduced private property. But above all it must be insisted that Vinoba's communism is by free consent.

As a disciple of Gandhi, Vinoba believes in the two fundamental principles of *satya* (truth) and *ahimsa* (non-violence). This makes his movement the exact opposite of Marxism. For by 'truth' Vinoba means, like Gandhi, obedience to the inner light and the voice of conscience, which is the voice of God; and by *ahimsa* he means that no violence of any sort may be used in the pursuit of his ideal. He demands the absolute renunciation of passion and selfishness, a renunciation which he himself learned from Mahatma Gandhi.

Vinoba goes even beyond Gandhi in demanding 'non-possessiveness'. He wants people to renounce the right to private property willingly, because they have overcome the desire for possessions in themselves. What is a Christian to say to this? It seems to me that we must say that Vinoba is asking for the fulfilment of the gospel, for that renunciation of property which the early Christians made when 'all the faithful held together and shared all that they had, selling all their possessions and their means of livelihood, so as to distribute to all as each had need' (Acts 2: 44). The only thing we can question is whether the average man is capable of this.

In India, and in the East generally, it must be said, this idea has a strong appeal. The people are much more communally minded, and sharing property comes easily to them. This is one of the reasons why communism has such a tremendous appeal throughout the East, whereas American capitalism with its emphasis on individual liberty and private ownership has little attraction. I have never yet met an Indian who did not repudiate the communist methods of violence and its doctrine of atheism, but the communal ideal, the idea of sharing goods in common and working together for the common good, has an immense attraction.

It is impossible to say how this will work out. One fears that Vinoba's idealism will prove too unrealistic and the communists will step in and take over with their ruthless methods. Yet may we not hope that the Indian village may succeed in taking the first steps towards a co-operative society, which is the true christian ideal?

A society based on the principles of the gospel, of faith in God, and non-violence, of common ownership willingly accepted; a society in which the individual renounces the exclusive right of private ownership and shares what he has with others, but is guaranteed what is necessary for the well-being of himself and his family; a society of free men organizing their life in co-operation and making themselves responsible for law and order – this is what Vinoba is looking for. He believes, like the communists, that in such a society the state would ultimately 'wither away' and a central government would no longer be necessary. Perhaps that is just utopian, but at present at least he has the full support of the state, and the whole system of education in India is being geared to this idea by the introduction of 'basic' schools, where village children are to be taught their lessons through the practice of some craft, and to have these ideals instilled into them.

I feel that a Christian can only look on this movement with the utmost sympathy and with the prayer that it may be blessed by God. One would like to see more Christians co-operating in it.

10. Walking with Vinoba

VINOBA IS the spiritual son of Mahatma Gandhi. Like Gandhi after independence, he has stood aside from politics and concentrated on the great work of *sarvodaya*. *Sarvodaya*, meaning literally 'service of all', is the name given by Gandhi to the movement which he began towards a new life in the villages of India. Vinoba, like Gandhi, has identified himself with the poor in the villages of India and his reason for walking from village to village is at once to help him to get to know the villagers personally and to place himself on a level with them. The organization which he has created is rudimentary, as he does not believe in organization, and the distribution of land has not gone very far, but there can be no doubt that he has awakened a new spirit of enterprise and co-operation.

What then is the basis of this new spirit he has aroused? I think that one can best understand it by reading a passage which Gandhi wrote in the periodical which he called *Harijan* many years ago. (*Harijan* means literally 'children of God' which, as we mentioned earlier, Gandhi called the untouchables, a name which has stuck to them ever since.) In this he wrote: 'Man's ultimate aim is the realization of God, and all his activities, social, political, religious, have to be guided by the ultimate aim of the vision of God. The immediate service of all human beings (*sarvodaya*) becomes a necessary part of the endeavour, simply because the only way to find God is to see him in his creation and to be one with it. This can only be done by the service of all (*sarvodaya*). I am a part and parcel of the whole and I cannot find him apart from the rest of humanity. My countrymen are my nearest neighbours. They have become so helpless, so resourceless, so inert that I must concentrate myself on serving them. If I could persuade myself that I could find him in a Himalayan cave I would proceed there immediately. But I know that I cannot find him apart from humanity.'

This passage is very characteristic. One notices in the first place how it is entirely in line with ancient Hindu tradition. For every Hindu the aim of life is *moksha*, that is 'release' or 'realization' of God, by which is meant an experiential knowledge of God as the one absolute reality. But what is profoundly significant is that this ultimate goal of life which was once sought in the solitude of a Himalayan cave, is now sought in the 'service of all humanity'. This is a mark of the change which has come over modern India. One can hardly doubt that this is due to the influence of Christianity. It is well known that Mahatma Gandhi himself was deeply influenced by the gospel, not only directly through the New Testament but still more indirectly through Ruskin and Tolstoy. Thus the social gospel of Christianity has come to be accepted in modern India and has been incorporated, one must say, into Hinduism.

But in the process this social gospel has undergone a most significant transformation. As is well known, the principle upon which Gandhi based his life and work was that of *ahimsa* or non-violence. Now this principle is deeply embedded in Indian tradition, not merely Hindu, but also Buddhist and, still more, Jain. It is held, in fact, that Gandhi owed his original grasp of this principle to the influence of Jainism on his childhood.

Where he showed his extraordinary genius was in his application of the principle of non-violence to social and political life. He applied it first in South Africa to obtain freedom for his people from the colour bar, and then in his own country to obtain the political independence of India.

In both cases, in spite of opposition which would have seemed overwhelming to anyone else, he met with final success. This has given the principle of *ahimsa* and the organized passive resistance to injustice which he called *satyagraha* an immense prestige in India. But in Gandhi's hands this principle developed into something far more significant than a method of passive resistance to evil. It became a positive 'soul-force', which he called the 'power of truth' and the 'power of love', and as such comes very near to what a Christian understands by charity.

Thus in an extraordinary way the principles of the gospel have penetrated into India and become fused with Hinduism. Indeed, one may go so far as to say that Gandhi has shown how the principles of the Sermon on the Mount can be applied to social and political life in a way which no one before him had done: he made the beatitudes a matter of practical concern in a way which few Christians have realized.

These are also the principles by which Vinoba lives and which he preaches in all the villages to which he goes. It can be seen from this that *sarvodaya* is essentially a religious movement. Indeed, one may say that Gandhi and Vinoba are engaged in preaching to ordinary people in the Indian villages the ideals of the gospel which the Church regards as counsels of perfection. Yet there is no doubt that these principles awaken a deep response. They have already a deep basis in Hindu tradition which make them congenial to the ordinary Hindu but at the same time they are given a practical application to the needs of modern India which makes them revolutionary. Vinoba asks that those who possess land share it with those who do not, and he appeals directly to the principle that the earth belongs to the Lord and that no one has a right to possess more than he needs at the expense of his neighbour.

In other words, what he is seeking is not so much a communist society as a co-operative society and in this he has the full support of the Indian government. At present it may perhaps be said that theories as to how the land should be held are fluid and that it has to be worked out by practical experiment. In any case, the guiding principle in all things is *ahimsa*. There is no compulsion in any form and it is always the villagers themselves in their assembly who decide how the land is to be farmed.

In all this, it seems to me, one can see the outlines of a genuine christian society coming into being. Between the extremes of individual ownership to be found in capitalism and of collective ownership to be found in communism, the christian ideal is surely that of a co-operative society. Such a society allows a great deal of flexibility in methods of ownership, but it is firmly based on the principle of non-violence. It consists in the willing co-operation of free men, who spontaneously renounce their rights of ownership in order to work together for the common good. This was the idea which was once realized in the early Church and, though practical considerations may make it difficult to realize in less privileged circumstances, it still remains a type of the christian ideal.

It is for this reason that I think that *sarvodaya* deserves our full co-operation as Catholics. It offers us a way of putting the gospel into practice in modern India, which may have great significance for the whole world. The western world is firmly rooted in a tradition of possessiveness with its inevitable corollary of violence in defence of one's possessions. The only alternative offered to this is communism with its concept of collective ownership, which means, in fact, complete state control and a corresponding policy of violence to obtain its goal. India is one of the few places where one can see a faint hope of a new order of society, based on non-possessiveness and non-violence, a society which might be able to correspond with the christian ideal.

The basis of this concept of society is, as has been shown, definitely religious, and represents a remarkable fusion of Hindu and christian ideas. Here, however, lies the difficulty, if not the danger, for a Catholic. The Hindu has very little sense of religious differences. He regards all religions as essentially the same in their basic principles, as differing only in their external expression of these principles, whether in dogma or in ritual. For him there is no difficulty about co-operating with people of different religions.

Gandhi, as is well known, introduced the custom of holding services in which there would be readings alike from the New Testament, the Koran, and the Bhagavad Gita, and in which prayers and hymns would be addressed alike to Christ and to Krishna and the other Hindu gods. A Hindu sees nothing inconsistent in this. For him Christ is simply one of the many manifestations or 'incarnations' of God in human history. He is quite willing to add also the Buddha and even Mohammed. It is not easy for him to understand the objections of a Christian to this view, and he is inclined to put it down to 'intolerance'.

This causes the real difficulty for a Catholic in co-operating in *sarvodaya* and it was this problem that prompted my visit to Vinoba. I was interested in starting a *sarvodaya* ashram which would be run by Benedictine oblates and would co-operate with the *sarvodaya* movement on a definitely Catholic basis. I thought that it was therefore necessary to get an assurance from Vinoba that we would not be required to compromise our faith in any way. For this I had to go to the far north of India, to a village near Agra where I found Vinoba encamped. The routine of his walks is now well established. He himself settles usually in the village school, which is put at his disposal and it was there that I found him.

In the evening he gives a talk to the people who have assembled from all the surrounding villages. On this occasion there must have been about five hundred people present, of whom about one hundred were walking in Vinoba's train. He himself looked surprisingly well and strong, considering that he was sixty-three at the time and has been walking in all weathers in India now for fifteen years. He wears the ordinary loin cloth round his waist with a shawl to cover the upper part of his body and sandals on his feet. When I saw him he was wearing a rather strange, American-looking green cap, which gave a touch of piquancy to his rather austere features with their white goat-like beard. This is, however, characteristic, for he is ready to use modern conveniences when they really serve a useful purpose.

I found at first that he was very much inclined to hold that we should not concern ourselves with our differences in faith, but should unite together in those common principles of 'spirituality', which belong to almost all religions. Indeed, I was told that he has recently gone further than this and has maintained that the different religions (or *dharmas*, as he calls them) should be decently 'buried' and that only their spiritual principles should be retained.

Against this point of view I maintained that there are real and essential differences in each religious tradition which affect their whole view of life and that we ought to respect these differences. It is not so much a matter of setting one religion against another, Christian against Hindu, as of recognizing that each religion has its own profoundly different point of view and that these should alike be respected. His objection to this was that religion then became a principle of division among men, which is exactly what we want to avoid.

I admitted that this was so to a certain extent, but I suggested that these differences are not necessarily final. We have to recognize that ultimately there can be only one

religion for mankind, but we cannot reach this one religion
by ignoring the essential differences which exist. What we
have to do is to strive to understand these differences and
through mutual understanding to work towards a reconciliation.

The time has now come, I suggested, when the different
religious traditions, Hindu, Buddhist, Christian, Moslem,
etc., which have grown up separately with little contact
with one another, have to meet in a 'dialogue'. The object
of the dialogue should be not so much to convert as to
understand one another and to penetrate more deeply into
the ultimate principles of each religion. In other words, what
we want is an 'ecumenical' movement corresponding to that
which is already taking place among Christians, by which
we may hope gradually to arrive at mutual understanding
and ultimately we may hope at world unity.

Finding that this point of view was quite acceptable to
Vinoba, as I think it would be to any Hindu, I went on to
insist that a Christian is bound to hold to certain principles
which he regards as essential to his religion. I mentioned
the doctrine of the trinity, the unique historical incarnation
in Christ, above all Christ as the one saviour of all mankind.
But I insisted at the same time that this does not mean
that a Christian must not respect other religious traditions
and strive to reconcile them with the truth of his own
religion.

Eventually I think I can say that Vinoba fully accepted
this point of view and agreed that a Christian should not be
expected to join in common prayer with Hindus when it is
against his conscience. Ultimately what is at stake is that no
one who works in the *sarvodaya* movement should be asked
to compromise his religious faith in any way.

We can work together in the service of God and humanity,
but we can only do this effectively if we hold fast to our own

religious conviction, while treating the convictions of others with an equal respect. This is surely a principle which holds for all multi-religious countries, and that is to say generally for the modern world. With this view Vinoba seemed fully to agree and I came away well satisfied that *sarvodaya* is in truth open to our full co-operation.

11. The Ideal of Non-violence

UNTIL NOW it has been a matter of debate whether it is legitimate for a Christian to refuse to fight, but now the question must be whether it is legitimate for him to fight at all. Even in the last war it was difficult to find a moral justification for the 'area-bombing' of Germany, and still more for the use of the atom bomb on Japan. But now the means of destruction have become so indiscriminate and their effects so far out of proportion to any conceivable 'just' end, that the whole concept of a 'just war' seems to be imperilled.

This, however, is a matter for moral theologians and ultimately for the Church herself to decide. But there is another aspect of the problem which should be of more serious concern to the individual Christian. Moral theologians tend to be concerned with finding how far it is possible to go in any particular direction without actually committing sin. But the gospel of Christ is not concerned merely with the avoidance of sin: that, on the contrary, is what in terms of the gospel comes under the 'law'; it is concerned to show the ideal of life which Christ sets before his disciples. In the Sermon on the Mount we have the christian ideal set before us in the most absolute terms, and this is the very essence of the gospel. It is not just a counsel of perfection given to a few chosen disciples; it is the call of the gospel itself, addressed to all men and summoning them to a new way of life.

At first sight these words strike us as an overwhelming paradox; they seem to be contrary to all normal human values. 'Blessed are you poor . . . Blessed are you who are hungry . . . Blessed are you who weep . . . Blessed are you when men hate you and cast you off and revile you, when they reject you as something evil for the Son of Man's sake. . . .' These are words which it is difficult even now for us to accept. Is not the whole philanthropic and humanitarian work of the world aimed at relieving poverty, hunger, misery, oppression, and here it seems these very things are praised? It is the same in regard to property, to marriage, to courts of law; Christ seems to call on his disciples to renounce all civil institutions. 'Unless a man will renounce his father and his wife and his children and everything that he has, he cannot be my disciple.'

There is a deliberate force of paradox in these words which warns us not to take them too literally, but at the same time they are meant to present a challenge to all our worldly values. Christ does not deny the value of civil institutions, of property and marriage and law courts; nor does he deny the need to relieve the poor and the hungry and the afflicted. But he wishes to assert that all natural institutions and all human values are of no account in comparison with the kingdom of God. A Christian may accept what this world has to offer; he may marry and possess property and defend himself at law, but he must be prepared to sacrifice all these things at any moment. We cannot exaggerate the radical renunciation which the gospel involves; we can never properly 'belong' to this world again.

It is in this light surely that we must read the words about non-resistance to evil, which strike us still more with the sense of paradox. 'But I tell you that you should not offer resistance to injury; if a man strikes you on the one cheek, turn the other cheek also towards him; if he is ready to go to law with you over your coat, let him have your cloak with it; if he compels you to attend him on a mile's journey, go two miles with him of your own accord. . . .' Christ does

not here deny the right to self-defence; he acknowledges
the right, but he calls on his disciples to renounce this
right. It is not a command; like the call to renounce marriage
and property it is a 'counsel'. But it is a 'counsel' which is
offered to all; it is part of the universal challenge of the
gospel.

This call, therefore, not to resist evil is embedded in the
very heart of the gospel. Like the call to renounce marriage
and property, it is part of the challenge of Christianity. This
is the conception which we need to recover in our present
situation. It is not a question whether it is 'legitimate' to
fight in a war, but whether the world has not reached a
point where we may be called upon to renounce this very
'right'. At least we have surely reached the point where we
must face this question seriously. We can no longer simply
accept war as part of a normal life. It has become something
so vast, so inhuman and so destructive that it challenges us
to ask whether there is not a way out, a way which is indicated by the gospel itself.

At present it must be admitted that the command 'Resist
not him that is evil' has become almost a dead letter in the
Church. We are sure that it does not take away from us the
right to self-defence and from that we go on to accept a
whole system of defence by modern weapons of war till the
gospel counsel ceases to have any meaning. In the same
way we know that we have the right to marriage and property, and so we put all our energies into building up a
world, based on these two institutions, which grows more
and more complex every day, until we almost forget the
meaning of the words, 'Unless a man renounce his father
and his mother and wife and children and all that he has, he
cannot be my disciple.' Thus there is the fearful paradox
that Christianity, which is based on poverty and non-
violence, has come to be identified in the eyes of so many
people with capitalism and war.

How has this come about? In the early Church there is no doubt that the sense of the urgency of the gospel was overwhelming. The first act recorded of the Church after Pentecost was as we have said that 'all the faithful held together and shared all that they had, selling their possessions and their means of livelihood, so as to distribute to all as each had need'. It is true that we hear no more of this experiment in common living and presumably the need of private ownership soon reasserted itself, but the gesture is significant. It shows the original impulse of the Church in regard to private property, and it was destined to endure and to take permanent form in the Church in the religious orders, which make the renunciation of private ownership the basis of their way of life.

In the same way we know that in the early Church, that is the Church of the first three centuries, the command not to resist evil was taken very literally. The Christians believed that they belonged to a new age, an age in which non-violence was now the law. So they boasted: 'We do not draw the sword against any nation, and we no longer learn to fight, because we have become, thanks to Jesus, sons of peace' (Origen). Military service was not forbidden, but it was not encouraged. It was not considered worthy of a Christian. His duty was not to fight but to pray, and it was thus that he could best serve his country. This was, of course, the attitude of a small community of Christians in the midst of a great empire, in which the regular army could be trusted to defend the country. The Peace of Constantine would change all that, and yet it retains its significance for us still.

But the non-violence of the early Church was carried further than this; it was carried to the point of death. The goal of life in the early Church was found in martyrdom; this was the consummation of the christian ideal. This is what gives its peculiar character to the early Church. The

Christians of those days were not afraid to marry and to possess property and to carry on business of all sorts, but they were made to realize that all these things might be taken away from them at any moment. They lived under the constant threat of martyrdom. And this was recognized not as something to be feared but as something to be desired. It was in this way that the Christian could best follow his Master. It was not by fighting but by suffering and death that he would overcome the world and establish the kingdom of God.

It is impossible to exaggerate the strength of this gospel of non-violence in the early Church. It was by this that the Roman Empire was overcome. The whole power of Rome was organized to crush this religion; yet it had to admit defeat and Christianity itself became the religion of the Empire. But this very victory brought with it a change. From this time the ideal of non-violence seemed to lose its power in the Church. Gradually the ideal of the 'martial' virtues, first of the Romans, then of the Gothic peoples, was substituted, and the ideal of christian chivalry was formed. There is no doubt that this ideal had its own beauty, but it belonged to a very limited period of history and was open to grave abuse. It was not an intrinsically christian ideal but an attempt to 'baptize' pagan virtues. The result has been disastrous; it has simply been the triumph of paganism. The christian nations have become distinguished above all others for their violence and brutality, and the very ideal of non-violence seems to have faded from men's minds.

There have, of course, been honourable exceptions, like the Quakers, who have preserved the ideal of non-violence down to the present time. But if we would see the force of non-violence in the modern world, we have rather to turn to India and to Mahatma Gandhi. It was he who, partly through the influence of the gospel and partly through that of ancient Indian thought, recovered the ideal of non-violence for the modern world. This ideal is basic in Indian religion and, one may say, in the Indian character. The Indian has always understood the true strength of character which lies in non-resistance, and it is this which makes an immediate appeal to him in the gospel. On the other hand, he is all the more shocked to find how little place it has in the life and thought of so many Christians. But it was the genius of Mahatma Gandhi which enabled him to discover in non-violence a means of political and social action which was found to be no less effective against the British Empire than the early christian action against the Roman Empire.

Maritain, in his *Man and the State*, has written of the importance of Gandhi's example in words which deserve to be quoted. 'In my opinion Gandhi's theory and technique could be related to and clarified by the thomist notion that the principal act of the virtue of fortitude is not attack but endurance; to bear, to suffer with constancy. One has then to recognize that there are two different orders of means of warfare (taken in the widest sense of the word), as there are two kinds of fortitude and courage, the courage that attacks and the courage that endures, the force of coercion or aggression, the force that inflicts suffering on others, and the force that endures suffering inflicted on oneself. There you have two different keyboards that stretch along the two sides of our human nature, opposing evil through attack and coercion, a way which leads at the last extremity if need be to the shedding of the blood of others, and opposing evil through suffering and enduring, a way which in the last extremity leads to the sacrifice of one's own life. To the second keyboard belong the means of spiritual warfare.'

This is surely a suggestion of great value to us today.

We need to recover this ideal of 'spiritual warfare', of a form
of non-violent resistance, which is specifically christian and
at the same time is the highest form of courage or fortitude
that can be found. It is, certainly, no easy form of virtue.
As Gandhi himself always insisted, it demands complete self-
conquest before it can become effective. In other words, it
is essentially a call to sanctity. It cannot be practised without
training and leadership. Gandhi spent all his life trying to
train his people for this, and in the end he had to admit
himself defeated. Yet it is something to which many people
feel themselves drawn. It seems to be the only way of giving
oneself wholeheartedly to a cause without seeing it ruined
by the use of unworthy means. Maritain has also spoken
of the need of a new type of sanctity today. May it not
be that we have here the means of such a new type of sanctity?

It is not, of course, a virtue which can be practised in
isolation. It has to be closely related to the other virtues
which constitute the christian ideal, especially to poverty,
chastity and obedience. In fact, it is among the religious
orders that one would like to see this ideal take the deepest
root, so that it is seen habitually as an essential element
in christian perfection. But it should not be confined
to the religious orders. It needs to be embodied in
social and political life and become a force of inspiration
there.

Communism, it is generally recognized, cannot be finally
overcome by force. Ultimately, it can only be overcome by
a spiritual force greater than its own. It has often been said
that Mahatma Gandhi was fortunate in having the British
to deal with, since they could always be trusted to observe
a certain code of honour, however ruthless they might be on
occasions. But would his methods have been of any use
against communism? In the same way, the early Christians

were able to overcome the Roman Empire, but again the Romans, although they were far more ruthless than the British, had not the communists' absolute ruthlessness and determination to eliminate all religion. Can a technique of passive resistance be found which can not only endure all that the communists can inflict but also convert them?

It may be said that communism represents the spirit of absolute violence. Violence belongs to its very essence: it arises from the nature of its creed. Materialism is of its nature a kind of violence to the spirit of man. It is an attempt to subject everything, and above all the human person, to the law of matter, and the law of matter is the law of violence. It seeks to impose itself on every form of spiritual life; it seeks finally to subject everything to the power of this world.

Non-violence on the other hand is essentially an affirmation of the law of the spirit. Gandhi described it as the 'power of truth' and the 'power of love'. It is the power of truth because it is the recognition of the spiritual ground of all reality and the determined effort to bring everything, that is, all matter, into subjection to this spiritual law. It is the power of love because it is the recognition of the spiritual character in every man and the inviolable respect which this demands.

Gandhi saw clearly that one must be absolutely un-compromising in one's attachment to non-violence. You can counter the absolute spirit of violence in communism only by a no less absolute spirit of non-violence. Once you allow any compromise to enter in, however legitimate it may be from another point of view, the whole strength of resistance is lost. One must be committed to the principle of non-violence utterly and completely to the point of death. The secret of the power of non-violence was revealed in the death of Christ. There was then revealed a love which was capable of bearing every insult and torture and, finally, death, without the least resistance, and which thereby raised up a new power of life capable of transforming the world. The secret of this power still remains within the Church; it is her secret, her hidden life. The Church and the world depend on our power to learn this secret and to show forth this life.

12. Non-violence and Nuclear War

IN DECEMBER 1960 a conference of the War Resisters' International was held at Gandhigram in South India, which I was invited to attend. I was only able to go on the last day, but I felt that the meeting was significant both for its timing and for its setting and for the conclusions to which it came. I was glad to find that there were two or three other Catholics present, including a priest sent by his bishop from Belgium. Catholics are not generally supposed to be favourable towards pacifism, but it is obvious that the threat of nuclear war calls for a radical change in our attitude to war, and it seems inevitable that there will be an increasing number who will feel obliged to take up a pacifist position in regard at least to nuclear war. The timing of this meeting was significant because the W.R.I. is an international organization without any religious basis, yet clearly it was felt that the birth of Christ was something which is relevant to the issue which faces all men today, and I must say that I was impressed by the spiritual attitude which was shown by the majority of the delegates. The setting also was significant because clearly it was felt that the country of Mahatma Gandhi was the country in the world which could best be expected to offer some guidance on the supreme problem which faces our generation.

There is no doubt that the Indian background gave a very definite character to the conference. It should be explained that Gandhigram is an institution founded some years after independence to perpetuate Mahatma Gandhi's ideal of life in India. It includes schools for 'basic' education, that is

education which is given through training in some form of
practical work from the earliest years, and schools for training in every kind of village industry.

It was interesting to find that the conference took the
two Gandhian concepts of truth and non-violence as its
basic principles and that it then went on to consider war
not as an isolated phenomenon demanding a particular solution, but as part of the problem of bringing a just order
into society. In regard to this it adopted the principles of
the *Sarvodaya* movement; thus the conference accepted non-
violence as the basic principle for human society, not merely
in regard to war but also in regard to social and economic
development. It is worth noting that it was led to declare that
'both the capitalist conception of private ownership and the
communist conception of state ownership ars insufficient
where the ideal of non-violence is concerned'.

This conception of an order of society based on non-
violence is surely something which deserves our serious attention. No one can pretend that a capitalist order of society,
even though it is superior to a communist one, can satisfy
the demands of a christian conscience. But the more closely
one examines it, the more clearly does it appear that the
order which Gandhi envisaged is essentially christian. It is
true that the idea of *ahimsa* is derived from Indian tradition,
not only Hindu, but also Jain and Buddhist; it is an ideal
which once formulated some five hundred years before the
birth of Christ, has gradually permeated the heart and mind
of India. There is no doubt, either, that Gandhi's first acquaintance with *ahimsa* was through the Jain and Hindu
traditions of his native Gujerat. But it is no less clear that
the reading of the Sermon on the Mount and the writings
of Tolstoy transformed this somewhat negative conception
into a positive dynamic force in his life, which he believed
was capable of transforming the world. He wanted to bring
out the fact that *ahimsa* is essentially a positive force. He was

strongly opposed to any idea of 'passivity' or failure to resist aggression. 'Non-violence', he once wrote, 'in its dynamic condition means conscious suffering. It does not mean weak submission to the will of the evil-doer, but it means putting the whole of one's soul against the will of the tyrant.'

Gandhi even went to the extent of affirming several times that he would prefer people to offer violence in self-defence than weakly to give in to an aggressor. But it was his deliberate conviction that non-violence was the better way to resist evil. He believed that moral strength is always greater than physical strength and that the man who gives way to violence is morally weak. But such moral strength he believed must be based on a complete freedom from hatred. 'It is no non-violence,' he wrote, 'if we merely love those who love us. It is non-violence when we love those who hate us.' He had no illusions about the difficulty of this, but he showed in his struggle with the British in India that he was capable of carrying it out in practice.

Again he was convinced that non-violence was incompatible with fear. 'We must give up all external fears. The internal foes we must always fear. We are rightly afraid of animal passion, anger and the like. External fears cease of their own accord, once we have conquered the enemy in the camp.' Thus it is clear that the discipline of non-violence is one which demands the overcoming of passion in all its forms, fear, anger, hatred, and also lust, for Gandhi believed that *brahmacharya*, that is chastity, whether in the married or the unmarried, was a necessary condition for a *satyagrahi*. He summed the whole matter up when he said: 'Non-violence implies as complete a self-purification as is humanly possible.'

Thus far it might be said that Gandhi was following the Hindu ascetic ideal, only making it of universal application and extending it to people living in the world and exercising their political rights. But there was a further element in his

conception of *ahimsa*, which seems to derive from the teaching and example of Christ alone. This was his belief in the
efficacy of suffering. 'The *satyagrahi*,' he said, 'seeks to convert his opponent by sheer force of character and suffering.
The purer he is and the more he suffers, the quicker the
process.' That this view of the mystical value of suffering
was derived from the example of Christ he showed clearly
when he wrote: 'I saw that nations like individuals could
only be made through the agony of the cross and in no
other way. Joy comes not out of the infliction of pain on
others but out of pain voluntarily borne by oneself.' We
have here, surely, the key to Gandhi's whole doctrine. He
had the courage to apply to the struggle for national independence the principle of suffering for justice's sake which
he saw to be the principle of the life and teaching of Christ.

It is this that gives Gandhi's teaching such an immediate
relevance to our own problems. For centuries the Church
has accepted the principle that violence is a normal way of
settling international disputes. Rules have been laid down,
not very successfully, to limit the degree of violence which
may be used, but few have had the courage to suggest that
the principle of suffering for the sake of justice, which was
proclaimed in the Sermon on the Mount and exemplified in
the passion of Christ, can be applied in the social and political
world. This was what Gandhi had the courage to do and
this was the method by which he won independence for
India. It is only recently that a serious attempt to face the
implications of Gandhi's teaching and action for the Catholic
in relation to the problem of war has appeared in Père
Régamey's *Non-violence and the Christian Conscience* (London,
1966). Here at last we have the principle of non-violence in
its social and political implications studied by a theologian
of note.

The reason why the doctrine of non-violence has so far
failed to penetrate the Catholic conscience seems to be that

the teaching and example of Christ in this matter are regarded as 'counsels of perfection'. They are not precepts
binding on all Christians but counsels given for the benefit
of a few chosen souls, which can safely be ignored by the
rest. Père Régamey shows what a caricature this is of Catholic
doctrine. The christian law is not merely a set of precepts
which have to be observed like the old law. According to
Aquinas the essential difference in the new law of the
gospel consists in the fact that it is an interior law; it is
nothing less than the grace of the Holy Spirit in the heart.
It is not merely a series of commands but a call to perfection.
'You shall be perfect as your heavenly Father is perfect' is
an exact expression of the new law. Every Christian is thus
called to perfection, to the love of God with all his heart
and soul and strength and to the love of his neighbour as
himself. The obligation of the gospel, as Père Dubarle has
remarked, is the obligation to respond to the love of the
heavenly Father.

Thus the sayings of Jesus in the Sermon on the Mount,
not to resist him who is evil, to turn the other cheek, to
give away one's coat, to suffer persecution for the sake of
justice, are not counsels given to a few, but the expression
of principles which must govern the life of every Christian.
Père Régamey further insists that these principles do not
apply only to the individual. Wherever there is a human
group which has been penetrated by the principles of the
gospel, the obligation exists to make these principles effective in public life. It is here that the fundamental principle
which guides all Père Régamey's considerations comes out.
Though the principle of non-violence, as expressed in the
Sermon on the Mount and in the example of Christ, must
be a guiding principle for all Christians, it will be applied
somewhat differently in the case of every individual and
every group of Christians. The principle of non-violence is
precisely not a law which can be applied indiscriminately on

all occasions alike. It is a guiding principle which has to be
applied by each person and each group of persons according
to their circumstances and according to their state of conscience.

Thus ultimately it comes to this: it is a matter of the
conscience of each individual person. There is no absolute
rule which can be imposed, there is only a guiding principle
and the inner light of the Holy Spirit to teach each person
how to apply it in his life. But what is essential is that this
conscience should be formed. At present it seems that very
little serious attention is given to this problem. The law of
non-violence, not to resist evil, to turn the other cheek, to
suffer for the sake of justice, to return good for evil, to love
one's enemies, is engraved in the gospel and was proclaimed
in a language which no man can misunderstand on the cross,
when God deliberately chose to overcome the powers of evil
in this world not by violence or resistance of any sort but
by suffering and dying. This was the example which was
before the eyes of the martyrs when they without exception
preferred to die rather than to offer resistance in any form.
This principle was so strong in the early Church that many
of the Fathers of the first three centuries regarded war as
incompatible with the profession of a Christian. The changed
circumstances of the fourth century led to a change in this
point of view, but the continuous tradition of the Church
aimed at imposing the strictest limitations on war.

Père Daniélou has also argued that the circumstances of
the present time compel us to re-examine our attitude to war.
Just as the conscience of mankind has developed on the subject of slavery and the use of torture, which were once not
only tolerated but authorized by the Church, so we may
think that the threat of nuclear war is forcing us to a deeper
awareness of the implications of war. It would seem that in
the teaching and example of Mahatma Gandhi we have an
extraordinarily penetrating light shed on this problem. The

christian conscience cannot continue to accept war on the modern scale as something which the normal Christian must accept as a duty, if he is called upon to fight for his country. It poses a problem for the conscience of every man, and the principle of non-violence as Gandhi conceived it is surely an essential element in the formation of a christian conscience. But if our conscience forbids us to take part in total war or in the use of nuclear weapons whose effects cannot be controlled, what alternative have we? The problem is particularly acute, because our potential enemy is one who threatens to impose a system of atheistic materialism on society, which is opposed to every christian principle. Yet it is here surely that our faith is most clearly tested. If we believe that Christ taught us to love our enemies, to suffer violence for justice's sake rather than to inflict it on others, to overcome evil by good; and if we accept his example in suffering and dying at the hands of an alien political power without resistance, in order to establish the kingdom of God, as the pattern of life, which every Christian has to try to follow; can we refuse to believe that this faith is capable of overcoming the powers of evil in the modern world? If we need an example in the circumstances of the present day to show what such a faith can achieve, we have again the example of Gandhi both in Africa and in India, where he was able to win freedom for his people in the face of the strongest political power by the use of non-violent resistance.

These methods of 'passive resistance' are still available to us today, as Sir Stephen King-Hall, for example, made clear. But if such methods are to have any force, as Gandhi so well understood, they must be based on a firm spiritual conviction. They cannot merely be produced in an emergency. It is here that it seems to me that the conclusions of the conference of the W.R.I. at Gandhigram are so significant. They were concerned, as I have said, not merely with resistance to war, but with the building of a non-violent order of society. Much discussion was devoted to the problem of easing tensions which may lead to war, such as racial conflicts, and it was decided to form a Peace Army, on the model of the *Shanti Sena* which Vinoba Bhave has founded in India, to attempt the work of reconciliation wherever conflicts may arise. Even more important than this was the decision to accept the principles of the *Sarvodaya* movement, so as to work for a social and economic order based neither on competitive capitalism nor on communist collectivism with their inevitable accompaniment of violence, but on free co-operation and non-violence. Such an idea may seem utopian, yet it is hard to see what other path is open to us as Christians. If we accept the principle of non-violence as part of our commitment to the following of Christ, then we must be prepared to follow this principle in every sphere of life. It is through the growth of such 'cells' of people committed to non-violence in their daily life, that we can best hope to establish the conditions of peace. It is for each to apply the principle in his own life as best he can.

13. *India and China*

NEHRU ONCE referred to the tension between China and India as a 'turning point in the history of the world'. From the point of view of the West there may seem to be some exaggeration in this statement, and yet if it is weighed in all seriousness, it may well be found to come very near the truth. The future of the world must depend very much on the development of Asia in the coming years, and China and India, with a population between them of over a billion people, represent more than a third of the population of the world.

But it is not only in the extent of their territory and the size of their population that China and India have importance for the world. They represent the two oldest civilizations of mankind, which have continued their history into the present century. The culture of both China and India dates from the first millennium before Christ, and both have had a continuous evolution until the present day. If we like to take a broad view of European civilization, we may say that it also dates from the first millennium, from the rise of Judaism and Hellenism, which combined their streams in Christianity to form the culture of Europe.

Thus there are three great cultures, covering the greater part of Asia, on the one hand, and all Europe with an extension in America and other former European colonies on the other. To them may be added a fourth, the islamic culture, which now covers the Middle East and a good part of Africa. This, though later in date than the others, has the same claim to be a universal culture, having its basis in a profound religious conception of life, and having shown itself capable of moulding human life in a form of civilization which has lasted over a thousand years. All these civilizations have this in common, that they were originally based on a common cultural tradition, which governed the economic, social and political life of the people on principles which were basically religious and were able to endure in a coherent form for more than a thousand years.

Into these ancient cultural civilizations there has broken in modern times the new secular, scientific, industrial culture, which took shape in Europe and America in the eighteenth and nineteenth centuries and has now spread to every part of the world. China and India only met the full force of this new way of life in the present century, and it is only in the last twenty years that it has come to impose its pattern on the whole of their way of life.

By an accident of history, or perhaps through some hidden cause which it is not easy to discern, China has received this new civilization in its communist form and India in its democratic form. Thus the fundamental conflict which has arisen in the West between communism and the democratic way of life is exactly reflected in Asia between China and India.

It is well to realize, however, that these two ways of life, communist and democratic, have much in common when they are placed in opposition to the ancient cultures both of China and India. Both alike are secular, scientific and industrial, while the ancient cultures of China and India were essentially religious, humanist and agricultural. Thus the impact of western civilization on China and India has been much the same. It has brought with it a totally new way of life, a new outlook, a new cultural tradition. The great difference is that in China it has been violently imposed with all the brutality of a totalitarian régime, while in India it has been introduced gradually, perhaps too gradually, so as not to disturb too much the ancient pattern of life.

It would be foolish not to admit that the Chinese way has met with some success. It has brought about a radical change in the whole economy of China and has engendered, at least in some parts, an enthusiasm which has effected a real social revolution. This social and economic revolution, in whatever way it may be introduced, is something which has to be accepted as inevitable. Even in the communist countries of eastern Europe there is now no more thought of going back on this. It is a new way of life which modern conditions are imposing on the whole world.

It would also be foolish not to admit that in India, where the tempo has been much slower, the process of change has been held up in many parts by the resistance of old customs which bar the way to progress. The caste system which still retains a tremendous hold on the villages, the old methods of agriculture which have scarcely changed at all in many parts, and the tendency to 'communalism', that is, to break up into groups based on language or race, or religion, which has endangered the unity of the country, have all slowed down the development of the new India.

Yet this very slowness has enabled India to avoid some of the disastrous mistakes of the Chinese. It is impossible to estimate what has been the extent of the suffering of the Chinese people, from famine, from forced labour and above all from the inhumanity of communism which is opposed to every tradition of Chinese culture. In India, though the government may often be inefficient and corrupt, it has worked with the people and in accordance with their cultural traditions, and though change may have been slow, it has been very deep. A new India is slowly coming into being which is modern in its economy and its social and political life but which still retains the basic traditions of the old India.

This is the real crux of the events which are taking place in Asia today. Modern industrial civilization, with its scientific view of life and its new morality, has disrupted the ancient civilizations of China and India. They are now in a melting pot. But it is certain that these ancient cultural traditions will gradually reassert themselves.

The Chinese will not for long be content with the crudity of a marxist philosophy. They are one of the most philosophical people on earth. The whole culture of China was founded on the teaching of Confucius, which was profoundly rational, humane and basically religious and which was above all a practical philosophy.

The Chinese have always been concerned primarily with social life. Perhaps this may be one reason why marxist philosophy has made a temporary appeal to some. Confucius was concerned to order the social and political life of the people, so that it would be in accord with the basic principles of the 'law of heaven'. As is well known, he made the family the basis of society and 'filial piety' the basis of all social relationships. No doubt this confucian philosophy had to be enlarged, and the conception of the mutual relations between 'heaven and earth' had to be developed in the light of modern science and democracy. But it is inconceivable that China should not one day return to this traditional philosophy, with its deep democratic principles, and reshape her life once more in its light.

In India, though the process of change has been gentler, the impact of modern civilization is hardly less devastating. While the Chinese is traditionally humane and practical, the Indian is essentially religious and contemplative. It is not for nothing that the mandarin, the scholar, was the principal person in Chinese society, while the Brahmin, the priest, had an absolute precedence over all other castes in India.

The position of the Brahmin, and the whole system of

caste which springs from it, have been rudely shaken in
modern India. But even more, the whole religious conception
of life, in which the life of the Sannyasi was held in the
highest honour, has begun to change. It is interesting to see
how the modern Hindu philosopher, like Dr Radhakrishnan,
tends to emphasize the reality of this world and the significance of human history in opposition to the view of the
Vedanta, which stress its illusory character. It is interesting
also to note how the influence of Vivekananda, who first
brought the idea of social action into Hinduism, has grown
through the Ramakrishna Mission; today the Hindu Sannyasi is expected to occupy himself with education and
medicine and social work.

But it was, of course, Mahatma Gandhi who was responsible for the most fundamental change in the Hindu attitude
to life. It was he who made economic, social and political
change something of vital concern to the ordinary Hindu
and thereby laid the foundations of modern India. Yet
Gandhi has become a problem for India today.

Gandhi's own mind was deeply religious and though he
advocated the most drastic changes in Hinduism, like the
abolition of caste distinctions, the emancipation of women
and a recognition of the absolute equality of all men, yet
his view of life was in many ways conservative. He always
thought in terms of a village economy and had little use for
industrialism. Above all, he based his whole philosophy
of life on the concept of *ahimsa*, which means literally
'not-killing', but with him came to mean something like universal love. It is this that has raised the problem in modern
India.

Gandhi is still revered as the Father of the Nation, and
his spirit, seen in his portrait, bust or statue, presides over
the community projects and development plans of the government. Yet in practice India has gone further and further
from the ideals of Gandhi. When Pandit Nehru set her on

the path of industrial development, though he himself remained deeply attached to the person of Gandhi, it was
inevitable that a radical change would come. Industrialism
brings with it the secular, scientific mentality, and India today has followed the rest of the world in this direction.

In nothing is this seen more clearly than in the attitude
to war. Gandhi was convinced that once India set herself on
the path of modern war she would betray her mission to
the world. Pandit Nehru tried to preserve this position for
India as a peacemaker among the nations, but the world
was too much for him.

A modern secular state with an industrial economy and a
modern defence force cannot hope to stand outside the
hazards of modern war. Goa was the first sign that Nehru
and with him a large part of India had renounced the ideals
of Gandhi; the more recent conflict with Pakistan seemed
to confirm this trend. With the China conflict, it seemed
that Nehru had practically the whole nation behind him in
his determination to resist to the bitter end. Indians seemed
equally united behind Shastri in the 1965 conflict with
Pakistan.

It is not easy to say what would have been the attitude of
Mahatma Gandhi to these two conflicts. Though he had
deep convictions and an unswerving determination, he was
a man of great versatility and it was never easy to predict
what would be his attitude to a particular question. Certainly
in India today there seems to be no question in the mind of
the people. The 1962 Chinese invasion and the 1965 Kashmir
crisis united the whole people in a determined will to
resist.

It may be that this will ultimately be for the benefit of
India. There has been a real danger in recent years that the
tendency to divide into linguistic groups and the conflict
over the question of a common language might lead to a
deep division in the country. Now it seems that the threat

to the integrity of the nation has brought the people together and given them a new sense of the unity of their
country and the need to preserve it. It is possible also that
the war effort, far from slowing down economic progress,
actually gave it more urgency.

Yet in embarking on a war effort India took a step in a
new direction and it is difficult to see where it will lead. The
old ideal of *ahimsa* still remains deeply rooted in the Indian
mind. Though the modern Hindu may accept the secular
state and the democratic way of life, he remains deeply
religious at heart. For many there is no doubt that this
presents an agonizing conflict.

In India, as in all Asia to some extent, the impact of
modern civilization has brought about a psychological conflict which it is difficult to resolve. Yet somehow a solution
has to be found. This is the real drama of the modern world,
which affects the West no less than the East.

The modern world, with its industrial economy, its political
democracy, its social emancipation and scientific mentality,
cannot be escaped. It is part, as far as one can see, of the
progressive development of mankind, as inevitable as the
changes which were brought by the discovery of metals in
the fifth millennium B.C. or the experience of the Greek
city-state in the fifth century B.C. Yet it has brought with it
a profound psychological conflict, both interior and exterior,
which threatens it continually with destruction. Of this
conflict modern war is only one symptom.

Somehow the modern world has to come to terms with
the ancient cultures which still underlie its structure. Whether
it is Christianity in Europe and America, Hinduism in India,
Buddhism or Confucianism in China or Japan, or Islam in
the Middle East, these religious traditions must be recovered
and become once more the guiding principle of political
and economic life. This is a problem for each religion. It

means rethinking one's religion in terms of the modern world, which presents a situation unlike anything known before.

The Church has begun to rethink her own position; and the movement of renewal which had been advancing steadily in the last ten or twenty years seems likely to take a definitive form as a result of the Vatican Council. Hinduism, Buddhism and Islam have also begun this work of renewal, and each has been able to present itself as a progressive and universal religion in the modern world. But the actual bringing of this religious point of view to bear on the problems of the modern world, such as war, has hardly begun. The Vatican Council had relatively little to say on warfare, and indeed it may be that the time is not yet ripe for this. It has become a question of conscience for mankind as a whole.

In the effort to answer this question one may hope and believe that India still has something to offer to mankind. *Ahimsa* is a deep, inward, spiritual principle, which has to be lived, as Gandhi attempted to live it, and only in the crucial experience of life can its meaning for the world be found. In the same way the Christian is called to rethink the principles of the Sermon on the Mount, not by any abstract theorizing but by the painful conflict of conscience, in which each individual has to face the demands of the gospel in his own personal life with its particular choices.

But ultimately we may believe that this problem will not be solved by any one religion alone. The time is coming when the different traditions of the world will have to draw together. No religion is static; each one has had a long process of growth, in which it has assimilated many elements from different quarters. We know that the Church has learned from Greece and Rome as well as from Israel, as Israel learned from Egypt and Mesopotamia. A renewal of Catholicism today cannot take place without a vital contact with the religious traditions of Asia. In the same way we may believe that Hinduism and Buddhism and Islam need the light of Christ. They cannot attain the full dimension of their faith, the term to which their evolution is leading them, without Christ. Christ is the head of all humanity, and the Church in her plenitude is the new humanity which is the term of the evolution of man.

PART FOUR

The Meeting of East and West

14. The Meeting of East and West*

DURING THE PRESENT century our western culture with its science and technology has penetrated into every corner of the Far East, so that there is scarcely a village in India which has not felt its impact. It is building up a new secular and scientific civilization, which, whether it is democratic or communist in its political and economic structure, presents an immense challenge to the Church and to every form or religion. It is the great task of the Church at the present time to confront this secular scientific culture, which is essentially the same wherever it appears in the East or the West, with the values of religion of which it stands in desperate need. But behind this conflict between religion and secular civilization there is a still more serious challenge which confronts the Church in the Far East. Here for the first time the Church is confronted with the ancient cultures of Asia, which represent the greatest spiritual tradition of mankind.

Yet it is only today that we are beginning to make any serious contact with the culture of the East. The Church came to Asia largely in the wake of the colonial powers and the Church was planted in India, not merely in its western Latin form, but specifically in its Portuguese form, so that not only western forms of art, but even social customs and (as a final insult) Portuguese names were imposed on Indian converts. Even for young Mahatma Gandhi, fifty years ago, being a Christian was associated with eating meat and drinking alcohol!

* Originally given as a talk at Santa Fé, New Mexico.

The cultural tradition of India and China goes back over four thousand years. They are the two countries in which the archaic culture of the ancient world has survived through a process of continuous evolution down to our own time. It is true that the impact of western civilization has in the last few years almost shattered this culture, yet its roots remain and in India at least there has been a conscious revival of the ancient tradition. Modern Hinduism is conscious of being the inheritor of one of the great spiritual traditions of mankind and even as having a mission to spread its teaching in the West.

This is what constitutes the challenge to the Church. These ancient cultures, especially that of India, are intimately bound up with religion; in fact, they are the expression of religion in all the different forms of human life, social, economic, political, artistic and philosophical. This explains, in part, the difficulty which the Church has found in coming to terms with these cultures. To make contact with Indian culture is to make contact with Hinduism and the attitude of the Church until recently has been that Hinduism is a false religion which is to be avoided like the plague by a Christian. It is here clearly that the most fundamental change is required. It is a question of how the gospel message itself is to be presented. As long as we try to present the gospel message as something opposed to the religion and culture of India we are doomed to failure. We have to learn to understand the Indian mind, its art and philosophy and above all its religious aspirations, and to present the gospel in its vital relation to this living tradition.

In other words, as in the West an ecumenical movement has taken shape in these last years by which we try to understand the traditions of our separated brethren, to discover not so much what divides us as what we hold in common, and then to relate our differences in a spirit of understanding and charity to our common faith; so there is need now of an ecumenical movement in religion, by which we seek to discover what is the common ground in the different religious traditions of mankind and then in the light of this understanding to comprehend all these different religious traditions in their vital relationship to the living Christ. This is the great task of the future. In a sense it is simply a continuation of the work which has already been begun by the Vatican Council. The Church has to renew herself in depth, to recover the essential form of her doctrine and discipline, purged of all the accidental accretions of the centuries, so that she may appear in all her universality, her essential catholicity, not bound to any particular form of language or culture, but open to all mankind, and able to adapt herself to the needs of human society in the East as in the West.

What are the lines which we may expect the Church to follow in this work of adaptation, or rather of incarnation in the culture of Asia? It seems to me that we have a very clear guide to this in the history of the early Church. The Church was born in the Middle East, as a small society in the Roman Empire, wholly Jewish in its culture and Aramaic in its speech. Within a few years after its beginning this little society was launched into the Graeco-Roman world, and we can watch the process by which in the course of five centuries it steadily adapted itself to this new world and became an integral element in the Graeco-Roman civilization, using Greek as its language and drawing to itself all that was vital in the culture of Greece and Rome. While retaining with fierce tenacity the judaic core of its doctrine and discipline and sacramental life, the Church soon abandoned Aramaic and took Greek as the language of the liturgy, while it did not hesitate to adapt its ceremonies to local custom and even to take its festival days from the pagan calendar. At the same time it developed its art and architecture from Greek and Roman models. Theology began with St Justin to use the language of Greek philosophy and by the fourth century

the whole of Catholic theology had received the impress of
the Greek genius. It is important also to notice how christian spirituality was developed by Clement and Origen and
later by St Gregory of Nyssa and Dionysius the Areopagite
along the lines of platonic thought. Finally the organization
of the Church was modelled on that of the Roman Empire
and the genius of Rome entered into its very structure.

Thus the Church of the first five centuries provides for us
a model of the development of the liturgy, the theology and
the canon law of the Church in the midst of a pagan environment, by which it was able to assimilate a new culture, while
yet retaining its essential form and message unchanged. In
the course of the next few centuries this tradition developed
along parallel lines in the East and the West, but now we see
an opposite process taking place. With the loss of the Syrian
and Egyptian churches to Catholic unity in the fifth century
the Church ceased to be open to new cultural influences. The
Greek and the Latin both hardened and became fixed. When
the western Church separated from the East in the eleventh
century it continued to develop along its own lines, until it
became finally fixed in the later Middle Ages. Thus it came
about that when the world of America and Asia was opened
to the Church in the fifteenth century it was a fixed form of
Catholicism, which was transplanted to these new lands and
no attempt was made at adaptation, except in some external
details. Ricci in China and de Nobili in India show us how
the Church might have been adapted to the culture of China
and India, but the forces of conservatism were too strong
and the experiment failed.

But while the Church was spreading westwards into the
Graeco-Roman world, it was at the same time spreading
eastwards to Mesopotamia and Persia. The language of this
Church was Aramaic (later called Syriac) and its cultural
tradition was wholly semitic. Its liturgy and theology and
canon law all developed on different lines from the Greek

and Latin (though it had close affinities with the Greek) and it constituted a distinct, though at first equally orthodox, christian world. It showed, moreover, a remarkable power of expansion and in the sixth to the ninth centuries spread all over Asia to China on the one side and India on the other. The rise of Islam and other historical circumstances reduced this once flourishing Church to the scattered remnants which survive in the Middle East today, but it has left one offshoot in South India, in which its liturgy survives among a large body of Christians, both Catholic and Orthodox (and also some Protestants) at the present time.

This Syrian Church in South India is of importance, because it provides an example of a Catholic Church with a distinctive oriental liturgy, springing from a christian tradition which is quite different from that of the Greek and Latin. Of course the Syrian Church belongs properly to the Middle East and its tradition is semitic, which is very different from the traditions of the Far East, but still it is an oriental liturgy which has become acclimatized in India and might form a stepping-stone, as it were, to a genuine Far Eastern liturgy. In the first place, like all eastern liturgies, it is open to the vernacular, and is in fact now celebrated in Malayalam, the language of the Kerala, in both the Syrian rites, eastern and western, which are used in Kerala. This use of the vernacular, which we are thankful to say has now been extended to the Latin rite, is, of course, the indispensable preliminary to the acclimatization of a liturgy. Once the vernacular has been introduced the way is open to the development of a native music, and experiments have already been made in the use of Indian classical music. Once the liturgy has become popular by the use of the language and music of the people, then one may hope that a sense of community will be awakened which will give birth to a distinctive form of art and architecture and so make the liturgy the expression of the life of the people.

The Syrian liturgy also gives us an example of rites and ceremonies, which are different from those of the Latin and Greek churches and in India in the marriage service, for instance, have adopted certain Hindu customs. But more than this it shows us a different style of liturgy, different in its gestures, its symbolism and its whole mode of expression. This is the really important thing, that a liturgy should correspond with the habits of thought and feeling and expression, which belong to the psychology of a particular people. Thus on the model of the Syrian liturgy, it seems to me, following the principles along which it has developed as an expression of a distinctively oriental form of Christianity, we could hope to see a living liturgy in the Far East, which would correspond with the cultural habits of the people.

Yet the liturgy by itself, though it places the Church, as it were, in the midst of the life of the people, cannot correspond to its cultural needs if it is not supported by a theology. It is here that the Syrian Church showed its weakness. The formation of the Syrian clergy is entirely along the lines of western theology and it is scarcely beginning even to take into account the tradition of eastern theology. It is here that the task in India is most urgent. Until the Church in India begins to take into consideration not only our eastern christian tradition but also the tradition of Hindu philosophy, we can hope for no real incarnation of the Church in India. Here also it may be that the tradition of the Greek and Syrian Fathers – particularly Dionysius the Areopagite who was a Syrian monk – would provide a bridge by which we could make contact with the Vedanta.

But the real task which awaits the Church in India is to construct a theology, using the philosophy of the Vedanta as its basis in the same way as the Greek Fathers and Aquinas used the philosophy of Plato and Aristotle. The Vedanta may be considered the greatest system of natural theology in the history of the world. Beginning with the Upanishads in the sixth century B.C., it has developed consistently over a period of two thousand years. Taking the Upanishads together with the Bhagavad Gita and the Brahma Sutras as its 'triple foundation', it was developed by a series of great masters between the eighth and fifteenth centuries into different systems, which have their schools and followers all over India at the present day. There is scarcely any aspect of theology which it does not take into consideration. It studies the nature of God and of man and of the universe; it has its own ideas of trinity and incarnation, of salvation and grace, of sacrament and sacrifice, of morality and asceticism, of mysticism and final liberation or beautitude. There is no treatise in Catholic theology which would not receive light from being studied in relation to the Vedanta.

The most important work which has been done up to the present time on this subject is that of the Belgian Jesuit, Father Johanns, called *To Christ through the Vedanta**. Father Johanns was a great Sanskrit scholar, who had mastered all the different systems of the Vedanta and studied them all in the light of the principles of Aquinas. His work was a pioneering effort, which needs to be taken up again, and there are in fact several scholars in India who are undertaking specialized studies on these lines. But the systematic study of theology in the light of the Vedanta has scarcely begun. What is perhaps the most important element in Father Johanns' work is that he indicated the lines on which a christian interpretation of the Vedanta should be made. The great problem which faces the masters of the Vedanta is that of the relation of God to the world, and I think that it can be said that this problem has never been resolved. The Advaita school of Sankara, intent on preserving at all costs the absolute purity and transcendence of the divine nature, is forced by its principles to deny the reality of the external world and to hold that God alone, the Brahman, really exists and that the

* See above, pp. 60–61.

universe of nature and of souls and even the personal being
of God is an illusion, that is *maya*. The other school of
Ramanuja, determined to preserve the reality of the personal
God and of the soul, is compelled to regard the universe and
souls as 'parts' or 'modes' of God, and so falls into pantheism. A third school, the dualist, or Dvaita philosophy, which
may have been influenced by Syrian Christianity (as its leader
Madhva came from Kerala) holds that God, the world and
souls are really distinct, but the world and souls are held to
be eternal, like God, and like all Indian systems it lacks the
idea of creation. This is the flaw which Father Johanns
found in all Indian philosophy; it lacks the idea of creation
and therefore can never resolve the problem of the relation
of God to the world.

Here then one may believe is the task of christian theology, by introducing the idea of creation, by showing Christ as
true God and true man, uniting in his person 'without separation and without confusion' the two natures of God and
man, it may bring the Vedanta to the goal which it has all
along been seeking. This would be not to impose an alien
theology on the Indian mind, but to show how Christ comes
to complete and perfect the age-long quest of the Indian
mind for the knowledge of God. Such a theology would
be a true conversion of the Indian mind to Christ, just as the
Greek mind found the culmination of its philosophical
quest in the theology of the Fathers.

Yet even so we have not yet reached the crucial point in
the conversion of India to Christ. Behind all the philosophical systems of India with their immense range of thought
there lies a profound mystical intuition and it is this which
has been the real inspiration of all Indian philosophy. Indian
philosophy is never a merely speculative philosophy; it is
always a way of salvation. What the Indian philosopher was
seeking was liberation from this world and the final bliss of
the knowledge of the Brahman. Now this knowledge is

essentially a mystical knowledge. The birth of Indian philosophy in the Upanishads came with the mystical experience by which the soul realized its identity with the Brahman. *Tat twam asi* – Thou art That – that is to say that the soul in the ultimate ground of its being is one with the Brahman, the ultimate ground of all being. This is the experience which underlies all Hindu religion and philosophy and which is sought no less earnestly today than at any time in the past. This is for the Hindu the ultimate experience in the light of which everything is to be known. 'When this is known, everything is known.' It is only when we have met the Hindu in this ultimate ground of his experience of God that we can hope to come to any understanding with him.

What then is the nature of the Hindu mystical experience? It has been analyzed by Maritain and other Catholic philosophers and its essential structure seems to be clear. It is an experience of the Self, that is the substantial being of the soul in its ultimate depth beyond sense and reason by an act of pure reflection on itself. We can catch the actual movement of the Hindu mind in this act of introversion in the words of the Kathopanishad: 'The Self-existent pierced the opening of the senses so that they turned outward; therefore man looks outwards not within himself. *Some wise man, desiring immortality, turned his eyes inwards and saw the Self.*' In these words one can discern the direction which the Hindu mind was to take for the whole course of history. Everywhere we see a movement of introversion, a deliberate turning from the external world, from the senses and the imagination and all that they have to offer, even from the world of reason in so far as it is based on the evidence of the senses, to discover the hidden source of Being, the root of the Self. The whole science of Yoga which is one of the six *darshanas* or systems of Hindu philosophy, is nothing but a scientific method of breaking through the world of the senses and separating the soul from its subjection to the body. In the ultimate stage of Yoga, that of 'seedless' *samadhi*, the soul is found in its isolation, separated from the physical universe and enjoying the experience of its own pure spiritual being.

It might be thought, and it has sometimes been said, that such an experience is unnatural and that it only leads to the soul's absorption in itself, but all the evidence of Hindu history contradicts such a view. It is clear that in this experience of the Self in the ground of its being the Hindu soul was brought into contact with God. Without images or concepts, but in the actual experience of its own spiritual substance the soul experiences the presence of God, the one, infinite, eternal, absolute Being, 'without a second' and this experience is one of absolute bliss. Such is the testimony of all Indian history. From the earliest texts of the Upanishads where we read of one who says: 'Friend, your face shines like one who has seen the Brahman,' to the recorded evidence of those who have known the great seers of modern times like Ramakrishna and Ramana Maharshi*, one can sense the reality of a mystical experience in which there is a pure consciousness of transcendent being in absolute bliss. I think that we have to take this experience with the utmost seriousness. There is something in it which is final and absolute. To the Hindu today no less than in the past this is the one, supreme reality for which everything in the world is to be sacrificed and compared with which everything else is of little worth. This is the secret wisdom of India, which sets her apart in the world and makes her the spiritual leader of mankind.

The trouble is that for the Hindu mind this experience of God has been so overwhelming that it has made it difficult for it to affirm the reality of this world. The world and the soul are lost in God. It is the paradox of Indian philosophy that whereas Greek philosophy starts from the reality of

* See below, p. 205 f.

this world and of man and leads to the knowledge of God, Hindu philosophy starts from the experience of the reality of God and seeks to establish the reality of the world. It is here, it seems to me, that the true meeting of East and West has to take place, and this is where in particular the Hindu mind needs to discover Christ. We have to show the Hindu in the light of our faith, that in this ultimate experience of God, the absolute being, the world and the soul are not lost, nor is the personal being of God absorbed in the impersonal Godhead. It is precisely in this ground of our being, in the real Self, that in our christian experience we discover the personal relationship which exists between ourselves and God and between one another. In christian experience there is a mystery of personal relationship even in the ultimate depth of the Godhead. The abyss of the Godhead, as it exists beyond all human conception, is not merely absolute being; it is a mystery of knowledge and love, of personal inter-communion of an incomprehensible kind, of which human communion in knowledge and love is a faint shadow. In the same way, our faith in the incarnation teaches us that the human and the divine nature are united in the person of Christ in such a way that the human is not absorbed in the divine, and in the mystical body of Christ Christians are united to God and to one another in a personal relationship of knowledge and love, in which while sharing in the divine nature, in the divine being, knowledge and bliss, they yet remain distinct in themselves, each a unique reflection of the being of God.

This, it seems to me, is our christian message to the Hindu. We do not deny in any sense what is ultimate in his experience of religion. On the contrary we strive in all humility to meet him on this very ground, to approach him as a brother who is joined with us in this quest of the ultimate meaning and goal of life. We have to accept his experience of the Brahman, of the Self in its ground or substance as an ultimate. But we have to show him that in this ground the world and the soul are not lost. They have to pass through a death and a resurrection, and in that resurrection they are found again, no longer subject to pain and death and corruption but participating, each according to its degree of being, in the very being of God. Thus the world and time, history and progress recover their meaning. There is a real creation, a real fall, a real redemption. Science and history both find their place in a real order of being, in which mankind is progressing, together with the whole created universe, towards a consummation, which will be revealed at the end of time. Thus Christ will appear, as Teilhard de Chardin has suggested, as the term to which the whole creation is moving and all the religions of mankind will be seen as preparing the way for the final manifestation of Christ. In this view Hinduism itself will be seen as a *preparatio evangelica*, the path by which the people of India have been led through the centuries of their history to their fulfilment in Christ and his Church.

But if Christianity can point the way to the fulfilment of the East, what have we in turn to learn from this encounter with the traditional religion of the East? It seems to me that the first lesson we have to learn is that of interiority. For centuries now the western world has been making staggering progress in the exploration of the external world, but the time has come when the balance needs to be righted, if we are to retain our sense of proportion, perhaps our very existence. We have to learn again to explore the interior world, to discover the other half of our soul, the ground of our personal being, in which is rooted our relation to God and to our fellow-men. The Catholic Church has, of course, a long history in the exploration of the inner world and the experience of God. But in these last centuries the Church has also felt the pull of the times; we have grown external in the practice of our religion, and to many people the discovery of the East, of Vedanta and Yoga and Zen, is a means of their awakening to the reality of the inner life. But more widely still, the Church as a whole is now engaged in a 'return to the sources'. We are seeking to recover the inner depth of our religion in the sources of the scripture, the liturgy and the Fathers.

Here, also, I believe that we have much to learn from the East. The study of the bible, the liturgy and the Fathers, can all remain external if it is not moved by an interior spirit of contemplation. If we would understand the bible and the liturgy, we have to recover the sense of the christian mystery, as the Fathers understood it. Now it is this, I believe, which the experience of the Self can give us. When we encounter God in the depths of the soul we encounter the 'sacred mystery', that hidden mystery which lies at the heart of all religion. It is from this centre that we have to approach the mystery of Christ in the bible and the liturgy, prepared to encounter God as Moses encountered him in the burning bush and Isaiah in the temple.

It is from this sense of mystery that we can also recover the sense of symbolism. It is the experience of Hinduism as of all eastern tradition, that when the soul has separated itself from the physical world and learned to know itself in the ground of its being in God, the whole universe appears as a symbol of God. Here again Hinduism tends to err in its interpretation. It finds the world not merely as a symbol of God, but as an actual manifestation of God, as identical in essence with the divine being. Yet though the philosophical formulation may be at fault, it expresses a profound sense of sacramentalism. The Hindu is not really an idolator. He sees the world 'charged with the being of God', and worships God in every manifestation in the created universe. To him everything in the universe is sacred; the earth and the sky, the hills and trees, the rivers and above all man himself. He has never lost that sense of the 'sacred', which Mircea Eliade has

shown to be the source of all religion. Surely we have much
to learn from him here. The western world has lost this
sense of the sacred. Our science which seeks to explain
everything by its causes, has lost the sense of their inner significance. It is so absorbed in the study of the finite, that it cannot see it as a symbol of the infinite. Yet such a sense of symbolism is basic to all religion. We shall never understand the
bible aright until we have recovered this sense of symbolism, as we find it in Origen and in the whole tradition of the
Fathers. Our new understanding of the bible from a critical
point of view is a necessary stage in our understanding of
the mystery of faith, but it has to be completed with the sense
of symbolism, the discovery of the mystery of Christ and the
Church, informing the whole narrative of the bible from
Genesis to Revelation.

It is from this point of view also that we have to understand the liturgy. The mystery which was manifested in the
mighty acts of God in the Old Testament is made present in
the sacraments and liturgy. Above all the mystery of the
eucharist, standing at the very centre of our christian life,
opens to us the whole world of symbolism. Here we learn to
see under the symbols of the bread and wine the whole economy of salvation, of creation and redemption and new
creation. If we could enter into the symbolism of the Mass,
we should understand how Christ is present in the whole
order of nature, drawing the universe into unity with himself, 'filling all things with his presence', as St Paul says.
Surely it is here that we must look for the recovery of christian art. All creative art, as Maritain has shown so impres-
sively, has its source in the hidden depths of the soul, far
beyond normal consciousness, where the soul is in touch
with the hidden 'mystery of being'. Creative art springs from
that deep centre, where the soul is known in the experience
of the world and the world is known in the experience of the
soul, as he has said, and for a christian this is the discovery

of the world and the self in Christ. Thus we are led back to that centre, in which the soul encounters God in Christ, and through him recovers the true understanding of the world of nature and the world of men.

As we learn to discover God in the centre of our being and of all being and thus enter into a living relation with all nature, so in this centre of being we find our true relation with our fellow-men. For in this centre we find Christ, who reconciles all men in unity with himself. We cannot now think of Christ except in relation to all men. He died for all and redeemed all and united the whole race of man, which had fallen in Adam, in one body in himself. Thus our faith in Christ teaches us to find his presence in all men. There is a hidden presence of Christ in every man calling him to union with himself and this presence is active in every religion and indeed wherever reason and morality are to be found. But we must add that if Christ is present to all men, then the Church is also present in all mankind. There is one movement of the Church which is visible in history, which we can trace in its progress from Jerusalem over the Graeco-Roman world, then over Europe and America and now about to enter into vital contact with Asia and Africa. But there is also a hidden movement of the Church going on in the hearts of men from the beginning, drawing men to Christ without their knowing it, in Hinduism, in Buddhism, in Islam, even in agnosticism and unbelief. It is only at the last day that the full significance of this movement will be revealed, but even now we can discern something of this hidden path of grace in the other religions of the world. Our ecumenical task is to co-operate with that mystery of grace, seeking to discover that presence of Christ in every religion and in every human soul. In this task we shall often find that we have more to learn than to teach, and that Christ has gone before us in the hearts of our brothers in religion. In the final meeting of East and West in Christ, who is to say which will gain the more, the Church, who will receive into herself all the treasures of the wisdom of the East in which Christ is already hidden, or the East, which will find all its aspirations fulfilled in him, 'in whom dwells the fulness of the Godhead bodily'?

15. The Church and Hinduism*

WHEN WE consider the number of conversions to Christianity in Asia over the last four hundred years, we must admit that the christian mission has largely failed. As soon as we ask why, I think we find the answer quite clear before us: the Church has always presented herself to the eastern world in the forms of an alien culture. A culture is the way people naturally express themselves; it embraces their language, music, art, even their gestures, their ways of thought and feeling and imagination. It is their whole world. In every case the Church has come to eastern people in an alien form.

In Bombay today one sees Gothic churches on every side, or sometimes a Baroque church, but never anything that is not reminiscent of western Europe. And they are furnished the way a church in London or New York might be furnished. One sees nothing that would make an Indian feel that this is his home, nor hear the language in which he would naturally express himself. I do not think one can exaggerate the sense of alienation which the Church creates in the eastern world.

Yet there are compensating features. There are always wonderful things in India. The first church where I stayed, though it had little to commend it in other ways, was packed with men, women and children in the doorways and in the windows, with the children clambering over the sanctuary. The Indians have a way of invading the set forms of the West and converting them into something wonderful of their

* Originally given as a talk in the Carnegie Institute, New York.

own. So, in a way, the Church has many Indian features, but in its church buildings, and of course in its liturgy, language and music – in everything in which it tries to express the gospel to manifest Christ to the Indians – the Church still appears as something alien. For example, the language of the Church in North India is Latin. Latin, however, is not even the language of all Europe, but only of western Europe. It is a particular language of a particular culture, and one might say of a particular age. It has, of course, a certain universality and usefulness at the present time, but when regarded as an organ of culture, Latin obviously has no place in eastern Europe, and certainly none in India or in China or Japan. It is as completely alien to the Orient as Chinese or Sanskrit would be in a mass offered every day in America. In India the Church appears western not only externally and in its language but in what goes with language, the mode of its thought. Because of the manner in which we present the gospel in the cultural setting of India, we are creating a barrier between the gospel, between Christ, and the Indians.

In what way then can the message of Christ be presented to the people of the East, which will be in accordance with their traditions? First of all we have to learn to respect these traditions. What we need today is an ecumenical movement towards the religions of Asia and perhaps of Africa, certainly with Islam, similar to the ecumenical movement which has begun among Christians. We know what a revolution has been brought about in a few years all over the world by the ecumenical spirit among Christians, partly through the example of Pope John, partly as a result of a movement which has been gathering in the Church for many years.

There is nothing to prevent our engaging in the same kind of ecumenical dialogue with the people of the East. I know from my own experience that the moment one shows an interest in Hinduism and some knowledge of it, the Hindu will immediately open his heart. That is the key to the whole Hindu world; without it all the doors are shut. There, it seems to me, is the way of approach for the Christian. I would say, too, that it has been one of our most impressive experiences in India that when Catholics and Orthodox and Protestants meet together with Hindus it is a wonderful means for thinking out our faith together, helping us to realize how much we have in common, and learning to present it in a way which can most easily be understood by Hindus. So, the two movements of ecumenism, towards Hinduism and among Christians, work together in a remarkable way.

We have to approach the Hindu in a spirit of friendship, with a desire for understanding; of course, this requires a considerable psychological sympathy on our part. We must get over a lot of western habits of mind and temperament, and learn to enter into the movement of their thought. Once we manage to do that we will begin to learn a great deal about their religion and the way is open for them to learn about ours.

In our dialogue with the Hindu certain changes in our mode of presenting the gospel are required. First of all, what is most natural, and what we can now at last see fulfilled, is, of course, the use of the vernacular in the liturgy. That is one obvious, indispensable preliminary step. As long as the liturgy is in a language which no one in India understands, its power of impact is almost nil. In India the majority is not literate, not in the habit of reading, will never, or rarely, bring a book to church. (I can remember saying mass in India conscious of the fact that no one else in the church had any idea of what I was saying. It was a humiliating experience.)

With the introduction of the vernacular, very naturally will come music. Where there is a vernacular language, there will be vernacular music. There is a wonderful sacred music in India which is only waiting to be adopted, and there are today some Indian priests who are adapting Indian music to christian themes in a very effective way.

But we have to go much farther than the liturgy. The Church has a perfect model of how it should proceed today in the way it proceeded in the early centuries. Christianity came out of Palestine as a Jewish sect. Yet within a few centuries this Jewish sect had taken on all the forms of thought and expression of the Graeco-Roman world. A christian theology developed in Greek modes of thought, as did a christian liturgy in the Greek language and in Greek modes of expression; a calendar also developed according to Greek and Roman traditions. Surely all that is a wonderful example, meant for our instruction, of how the Church can present herself to an alien world, receiving forms into herself while retaining integrally her own Catholic message.

In this early Church there were various groups of Christians who did not speak the common language, which at that time was Greek; when the Church came to villages where Greek was not spoken it took up Syriac, or Coptic, the Egyptian language, or some other vernacular, and the bible and the liturgy were translated into it. The Church in India cannot stop short at a semitic liturgy, with a semitic language, which is after all what the Syrian liturgy is. Indian Christians must hope for a truly Indian liturgy, but first the Indian tradition of thought must be taken into account.

India has a wonderful tradition of philosophy and theology which has been developing for centuries; it is truly one of the great traditions of mankind. Our work must be to do for Indian philosophy what Augustine, the Greek Fathers and Aquinas did for Greek philosophy: bring it into the life of the Church. To do that we will have to learn to express christian theology in terms of the Vedanta. This surely will be one of the great ecumenical tasks of the future.

But there is something more. The Indian, the Hindu in particular, is not concerned simply with learning about God. His great concern is to discover God, not to know *about* him, but to know God himself, to have the experience of God in his life. Very often in India someone has come up to me and asked, 'Have you realized God?' by which he meant, 'Do you know the presence of God in your life?'

For the Hindu, this experience is fundamental; to him it is the ultimate experience. All through Indian history there has been this yearning to experience God in the depths of the soul. The whole system of Yoga, with all its discipline of *āsana* (posture) the *prāuāyamā* (breathing), the control of the senses and the mind, is intended to bring the heart and the mind into a state in which it can, in the Hindu view at least, be absolutely one with God, with the 'ultimate reality'. To the Hindu this is the ultimate experience, and it is as living in India today as it ever was in the past. That is where our christian contact finally has to take place. To meet on the level of liturgy, of language, music and art, is not so difficult. To meet on the level of philosophy and theology is a difficult and extended task, though I think we can manage it eventually. But to meet in the interior depths of the soul, in this experience of God, is, I believe, the final task of the Church, not only in India but in all the East, because this experience is common to Hinduism, Buddhism and to a large extent to Taoism. It goes right through the oriental tradition. Even those orientals who are westernized and who have adopted western habits of thought, still have in their hearts the awareness of an inner reality, which western people have so largely lost. In the West many people are turning to Hinduism, Buddhism and Zen Buddhism in particular, because they are seeking this experience which they do not find in their own lives, and very often do not find in Christianity. That is not necessarily the fault of

Christianity, but it is perhaps symptomatic of the way Christianity is presented to us today.

This thirst for a spiritual experience can easily become cheapened and can take all sorts of fantastic forms; yet there is something very deep and sincere behind it. Our very success in the material world, in building up a great civilization, has left us with a sense of frustration in human life, a feeling of emptiness within, a lack of reality, an inability to touch the inner centre of being where we are at rest and where we can go out to meet our fellow-men, go out to meet God, but to which we can always return.

It is this centre we have to find in the West; the Hindu and the Buddhist have been seeking it all through the centuries in the East, and in a very real sense they have the secret of it. It is said that in this experience of non-duality, *advaita* as the Hindus call it, a point is reached where differences disappear. It is the inner centre where one is united with God, the ultimate reality. This Hindu experience, though it has various interpretations which may not be altogether adequate, is a very great thing. Jacques Maritain and other philosophers have explained it as ultimately an experience of the soul in its inmost depths; through it we get beyond the world of the senses, beyond our imaginations, beyond all the world of thought which always occupies us, until we reach the inner centre where the soul is resting in itself. Maritain calls it an 'experience of the substantial being of the soul', the soul in its ground of reality. That surely is something very real and I think many of us have an unconscious desire for it.

But I think this is important: the experience of the soul in its depths is not an experience of the soul alone; indirectly at least God is encountered, the source of life, the source of being. Therefore, this Hindu experience (which the Buddhists also have, though in a somewhat different formulation) is really an experience of God in the sense of an experience of the absolute, the infinite, the eternal. In reading the ancient Buddhist or Hindu books, one gets a sense of a genuine mystical experience. Passing beyond the barriers of the finite, the relative, and the temporal, the absolute is reached. That surely is something of immeasurable importance. What is lacking in our life today, in Europe as much as in America, is precisely this inner dimension, an experience of the absolute, which used to be fundamental. When one looks at some ancient Hindu temple, or a sculpture of the Buddha sitting in contemplation, or even simply at a Chinese vase, one finds a tranquillity, a depth, which arises from a centre of being. It was conceived from this inner centre and arose creatively from it.

The Hindu, the Buddhist, the oriental, have this experience of an inner reality and it is very deeply related to the experience of God, though they may not call it that. The Buddhist will express it in a negative way, calling it Nirvana, or the blowing out, the passing away of the relative and the temporal, reaching the absolute. The Hindu conceives of it as a discovery of God, the Brahman, the one eternal Being, but also very often as the discovery of a personal god. Here we come to the crucial point. We as Christians are seeking for this interior experience of reality, of depth, of a centre to our life, and I believe that the Hindu and the Buddhist can help us very much – not so much by techniques, although some may find those helpful, but by the whole orientation of their thought towards the centre of inner reality. They can help us to reach it, but I would say very strongly that here we, as Christians, have something which they have not, because the weakness of Hindu thought from the beginning has always been that it has never been able to find a true relation between God, or the Absolute, and the relative world of time and space. Here I believe is the core of the christian message to the East.

Hindu doctrine practically divides into two streams: one

is the *jñāna mārga*, or way of knowledge, taught by Sankara*, a doctor of the eighth century, who, while maintaining that the Absolute is one, eternal, infinite, unchanging being, knowledge and bliss (a perfect conception of God in the natural order) was compelled to say that the world itself is *maya*; it has no reality in itself. Therefore, this world, and all the life of human beings in it, has no ultimate reality. The one ultimate is the Brahman, the infinite.

In reaction to this, Ramanuja† in the eleventh century, and the school which followed him, tried to retain the reality of a personal god, of this world and of their own souls. Their school of thought, called *bhakti-mārga*, which means the way of devotion, held that there are real distinctions. But not having any proper idea of creation, of the real relation between this world and God, they said that the world and souls are parts of God. Thus, there are these two extremes of what is sometimes called monism, and of pantheism in which all ultimately is divine, is part of God. Christian doctrine stands in between: to my mind it brings the Vedanta and all Indian thought to its fulfilment. It shows that in this centre we do not lose the world, we do not lose our fellow men, we do not lose a personal relation to God. On the contrary we find them, because in this centre we make a personal contact with Christ, who himself is God in person. Therefore, in the centre to which the ecumenical relation with the Hindu should bring us, we should be led to a deeper understanding of our personal relation to Christ in the depths of our souls. From that relation to Christ we reach a personal relationship with God, with the Father, with the Holy Spirit. Our whole christian experience is an unfolding of relationships of knowledge and of love. That, to my mind, is what the Hindu is really seeking.

A study of their texts would reveal that that is what they

* See below, p. 202.

† See below, p. 215.

have in mind. They are seeking it all the time, but with the material they have and without the light of revelation, they have not been able to reach it. Consequently, I would say we are not simply bringing a new religion to India. We are discovering in the depths of Hinduism its inner dynamism, its inner movement towards fulfilment, which will be found in Christ. That surely is to preach the gospel in the very heart of Hinduism, as it were, in answer to its deepest desires.

Not only do we find this personal relationship to God; we also find it to one another. Instead of losing ourselves in God or the Absolute, which is the tendency in Hinduism and still more in Buddhism, we find ourselves. In that inner depth we reach a personal relationship with one another. We discover the mystery of the person: that we, each of us, are unique manifestations of God; that is what creation means, that God gives to each one of us a being which is unique, which is eternally related to him and which has the purpose of final fulfilment in him. When we reach personal relationships with one another, our whole being is open to the world of creation.

That seems to me to place Christianity in the very centre of eastern doctrine, and to be the way the East and West can gradually meet in Christ. Once we begin to see Hinduism, Buddhism and other religions in this light, once we begin to see that they themselves are moving towards Christ, then it gives us a different idea of the place of all these religions in relation to Christianity. I feel that is fundamental. We cannot go on simply taking a negative attitude towards Hinduism, Buddhism or 'pagan heathenism'. We have to take a positive attitude; and here I would like to mention a very remarkable book by R. C. Zaehner called *The Convergent Spirit*; in it he develops the idea of Teilhard de Chardin of the convergence of all creation on Christ.

Teilhard de Chardin's idea is really the idea of Paul, that

the whole creation from the beginning – all things in heaven
and earth – converge upon Christ. They come to their fullness, to their head in Christ. Zaehner makes a further point,
which seems to me to follow necessarily, that all religions
converge on Christ, that there is a movement towards Christ
in all religions.

In other words, the mystery of Christ which we find in
our religion is present in all religions in an embryonic form
from the beginning. When we go to preach the gospel, we
are not therefore presenting a new gospel so much as discovering the hidden presence of Christ at work in all different religions and among all different people. Is this not
really the essence of the ecumenical approach – that we approach our brother as someone in whom Christ is already
present, imperfectly, embryonically perhaps but nevertheless there? Always we are going out to Christ in him, and
we are ready to learn from him before we begin to teach.
This is a new attitude in a sense, but one which flows inevitably from the ecumenical movement and from a consideration of the actual nature of the different religions as they
exist today.

I would like to see the spirit of ecumenism enlarged so
that we can look out on the world and see that the mystery
of Christ, which we try very imperfectly to realize in our
lives, is hidden in all ancient religions. It is the mystery of
God which was present from the beginning. There has
never been a time when God's grace, when his Spirit was
not present in mankind, leading men towards the truth. The
mystery of Christ is present in all religions from the beginning, and that means the mystery of the Church is present in
all religions from the beginning.

That certainly should change our approach to all these
different religions, and should have a deep effect on our own
lives. We have to admit that though the fullness of truth is
always present in the Church, yet it is not present to any in-

dividual Christian. We as Christians have an imperfect understanding of the mystery of Christ at any time. But we can reach a deeper understanding of it through contact with our Hindu and Muslim brothers, our Buddhist and Jewish brothers and any others one can mention, even if they are atheist brothers, because an atheist often is one who is really seeking God, or the truth, and has only rejected a false conception of God. No one can ever judge in any man what the fundamental movement of his soul is. Wherever we encounter such people we are encountering Christ. That is how the Church has grown: through contact with Graeco-Roman religion there was the wonderful expansion of the early centuries; through contact with the barbarian peoples of Europe (the Teutons and all the rest) there was the growth of the Middle Ages. On the other hand, there has been, on the whole, a contraction of religion in the last five hundred years due to the conflicts among Christians. But the world of the Middle Ages is over and the world of the Counter-Reformation, of Catholic against Protestant, is slowly but surely dying. We are entering into a new world in which we are, for the first time, brought into contact with the new nations which are rising on every side. What I have said about India naturally must be extended to all the peoples of Asia and Africa, who are becoming conscious of their cultural heritage, of their rights as human beings, of their place in the world.

Surely the Church must have a message for this new world. It cannot simply continue with the forms of Graeco-Roman culture of medieval law and theology. We have to enter into this wonderful new world which is being born before our eyes. We as Christians, and I would say above all as Catholics whose religion is, by definition, universal, belong by right to all these different cultures. But we should see that not only have we something to say to them, they have something to say to us.

I do not know what wonders the different African cultures may have to give to our liturgy in the way of music or of dance, for instance, or in other different forms of art. Even more evidently the people of Asia are able to bring to us a wonderful contribution in philosophy, theology, and above all in mysticism. Can we not as Catholics open our hearts and our minds to this new world, approach it in an ecumenical way, ready to find Christ there, ready to respond to Christ in them and very humbly ready to witness to Christ in ourselves? That is what the Hindu wants to see. As I have said, he is always asking, 'Have you realized God?' Only when he sees christian Sannyasis who have made the renunciation which he understands, who have discovered God in the depths of their hearts and are living from that contact – only then will he recognize Christ in his true form in India. Then I believe that the love and devotion which the Hindu would give to Christ would perhaps be beyond anything – certainly equal to anything – that we have known in all the history of the Church.

Because the more one knows Hinduism, the more one realizes what wonderful resources of great, of true religion are present there. I do not think it is too much to say that they can only find the fullness of that religion in Christ. We need not impose Christ or the Church on them. We need only ask them to meet us in a living approach to Christ, to God, to find their fulfilment with us in that Church in which all mankind will eventually be reconciled in Christ.

16. The Salvation of the Unbeliever

WHEN ONE lives in a country of nearly 450,000,000 inhabitants, of whom not more than 2 per cent are Christians and 1 per cent Catholics, the problem of the salvation of the unbeliever is something which is continually before one's eyes. But it is not only in India, or the Far East as a whole (where the proportion of Christians is even less), that this question is forced upon the mind. It seems to me that it is one of the most urgent problems, if not *the* most urgent problem which faces a Christian everywhere today.

On the one hand we believe that Christ is the only saviour of mankind. As St Peter said at the very beginning of the Church's history, 'there is no other name under heaven given to man by which we must be saved' (Acts 4: 12). On the other hand we believe that the Church is the mystical body of Christ, and is thus identified with Christ, so that outside the Church there can be no salvation. And yet, if we confine our attention to the visible Church, we see that after nearly two thousand years only a minute section of humanity has any apparent connection with the Church. Not only, as we have said, is the Far East still scarcely touched by Christianity, but the Middle East, the very place where the christian religion rose and which was once the most christian part of the world, is now almost entirely subject to Islam, while Africa, though it has the beginnings of a new Christianity, is still largely pagan or Muslim. Even if we turn to Europe, of which Belloc once proudly said, 'Europe is the Faith', we find that whole countries which were once christian have either ceased to be so altogether or remain

so only in name. Let it be added that the number of 500,000,
000, which is usually given for the Catholic population of
the world, is largely illusory. It includes all those who are
baptized as Catholics, but if we ask how many are practising Catholics, we should have to reduce it by half, if not
more.

Thus if we take the world as it is today and consider the
number of practising Catholics, or even practising Christians of any kind, the Church appears as a small minority.
But if we look back in time, the position is even more serious.
Christianity began as the religion of a small group of people
in the Roman Empire. In the course of centuries it became
the religion of the greater part of the Roman Empire, and
even of some countries beyond, but it never touched
the greater part of the world. For a thousand years after
this it remained practically confined to Europe. Then
in the sixteenth century it had an extension to America
and to other places which were colonized by Europeans,
but the world beyond these boundaries still remained untouched.

Thus even if we confine our attention to the small por-
tion of historical time, in which it has actually been in existence, Christianity cannot claim at any time to have been a
universal religion. But if we look back further in time, the
position is much worse. As long as it was believed that the
world had been in existence for about 5,000 years, and that
the bible gave a summary of human history, the comparatively late appearance of Christianity could be explained
without much difficulty; it represented the last phase in a
religious development which could be traced from Adam,
through Noah, Abraham, Moses and the prophets to Christ.
But now that we know that man has been on earth for hundreds of thousands of years, the relation of these untold
millions of people, scattered all over the globe, to Christ and
the Church becomes a serious problem.

It is possible to approach this problem from different points of view, but the one I have found most helpful is that of Father Daniélou in his little book *Holy Pagans of the Old Testament*. The value of this approach is that it is from the point of view of divine revelation itself; it is the way in which the salvation of man is actually presented to us in the scriptures. The purpose of Father Daniélou is to show that the Old Testament itself recognizes the existence of a whole series of holy men, who are in fact regarded as 'saints' by the Church, who were in reality pagans. These holy men are found in all the generations from Adam to Abraham, and include Abel, Seth, Enoch, Noah, Melchisedec and Lot, while after this time there are to be found the interesting figures of Job and 'Daniel', the original perhaps of the prophet of that name, who appears to have been a pagan.

The significance of this is that according to biblical doctrine the salvation of man has never been confined to Christians or Jews. It was open from the beginning to all men and for the first three thousand years of human history, even according to biblical reckoning, the 'saints' of the Church were pagans. It is true, of course, that we have to revise biblical chronology drastically. Where it reckoned in thousands of years, we have to reckon in hundreds of thousands. But the principle remains the same. God's plan of salvation from the beginning of the world included all men on the face of the earth. These people also, as Father Daniélou shows, were the subjects of a 'covenant' with God, to the first covenant with Adam, or to the second covenant with Noah.

Now what was the nature of this covenant? It is here that Father Daniélou makes an important point. This covenant may be called the covenant of the natural law, but this does not mean that early man had no other way but that of 'natural reason' to know God. The covenant of the natural law was a supernatural revelation which Father Daniélou calls the 'cosmic revelation'. It is the revelation which God makes through nature and the human conscience, of which Paul speaks in the Epistle to the Romans, but though it comes through nature and conscience, it is not the product of reason. It is a covenant of grace, by which God reveals himself as the object of a supernatural faith.

What was the content of this revelation? Its basic requirements are found in the Epistle to the Hebrews, where it is said: 'He who comes to God must believe that God exists and that he rewards those who try to find him' (Heb 11: 6). It is interesting to find that this is the text which Aquinas takes when he wishes to show how it was possible for those who lived before the coming of Christ to be saved, and maintains that to believe in God and to trust in his providence is implicitly to believe in Christ, because 'belief in providence includes all the temporal dispensations of God in view of man's salvation' (S.T. iia-iiae, 1,7). Thus we may say that the cosmic covenant already contains implicitly the revelation of God's saving purpose in Christ. Those who were saved under this covenant were saved by their implicit faith in Christ and were therefore properly members of the Church of Christ.

This is surely a principle of immense value when we ask ourselves what is the position of the 'pagan', that is all those who are apparently outside the special covenant, which God made first with Israel in the Old Testament, and then with the Church in the New Testament. These people are not 'unbelievers' in the proper sense. They are subjects of the original covenant of God with man, believers in the cosmic revelation, which is given through nature and conscience and is open to all mankind. The study of comparative religion has shown how this faith lies behind all primitive religion. Mircea Eliade, in particular, in his *Patterns in Com-*

parative Religion, has shown how belief in the Supreme Being, the Sky God or 'Father in heaven' and the moral law which derives from it, can be found in the religion of primitive people all over the world, in Asia, Africa, Australia and America, and how it appears also in the background of all the great historic religions, of Egypt and Mesopotamia, of China and India and Persia. We can speak therefore of a religion which is universal, a witness to the true God, which is present at all times and in all places.

It is true, of course, that this original basis of all religion is often obscured; the supreme God tends to become a *deus otiosus* and gives way before more dynamic and earthly gods, yet it is remarkable too how his presence seems never to be wholly lost. In the great religions of the world today, in Hinduism and Buddhism, and still more evidently in Islam, this presence of God is particularly evident. In Hinduism, from its very earliest history, we can see the Indian mind continually rising above the multitude of gods to the one supreme Being, and even conceiving an idea of grace and incarnation. Buddhism presents a problem in a sense, because it is often called 'atheistic'. This is true in the sense that Buddhism at least in its primitive form does not recognize a personal God, but the faith of the Buddhist is nevertheless in the supernatural. Nirvana is, almost by definition, a supernatural state, transcending both sense and reason, and the faith of the Buddhist is mediated by the figure of Gautama, who is of all religious leaders the one who in his moral stature comes nearest to Christ. Islam belongs, of course, to a different category from Hinduism and Buddhism; it belongs to the semitic group of religions, and depends to a considerable extent on the revelation of the Old Testament with some influence also from the New. Yet basically it may be said that Islam is a perfect example of the cosmic revelation. It is a magnificent expression of faith in the one creator God and his providence, without the distinctive characteristics which mark the Hebrew and christian revelation.

Thus I would say that Hinduism, Buddhism and Islam all come under the cosmic revelation, the primeval Covenant of God with man. No one can say in a proper sense that the Hindu, the Buddhist or the Muslim is an 'unbeliever'. I would say rather that we have to recognize him as our brother in Christ. Though he has not received the revelation of God in Christ, and may even, like the Muslim, have rejected Christ owing to a false and superficial knowledge of him, which was all that Mohammed possessed, yet he has a genuine faith in a supernatural order, and Christ, though hidden from him, is surely present to him by his grace.

A problem arises, however, over those who have more or less consciously rejected Christ, like the atheist and agnostic of modern Europe and America. What are we to say of them? It seems to me that Maritain gave the answer to this problem, when he said that a man is to be judged not by the explicit, conscious rational form of his belief or unbelief, but by the fundamental orientation of his intellect and will towards truth and goodness, which is ultimately known only to God. Thus there are many people who are atheists or agnostics because they have rejected a false and unworthy conception of God or of Christ or the Church, because their conscience and their very desire for truth and goodness led them to do so. Not every atheist or agnostic, no doubt, is in this position, but as we have said, of this God alone is the judge. What we can say with certainty is that at all times and in all places God (and that means Christ) is soliciting the heart and mind of every man through his reason and conscience, and all alike, believers and unbelievers, are to be judged by this hidden call of grace and their response to it.

We thus reach the rather paradoxical conclusion, though it is theologically certain, that it is not by his outward profes-

sion of faith, whether he is Christian or Jew, Hindu, Buddhist, Muslim, agnostic or atheist, that man is saved, but by
his response to the call of grace, which comes to every man
secretly in every religious or irreligious state. Of course, it
remains true, as we believe, that greater opportunities of
grace are given in the christian religion, and in the Catholic
Church, but on the one hand no one is excluded from this
covenant of grace, and on the other hand we know that 'to
whom much has been given, of them much will be required'.

Perhaps this may provide an explanation of the rather mys-
terious saying of the gospel: 'If anyone shall deny the Son of
Man it shall be forgiven him, but if anyone shall deny the
Holy Spirit, it shall not be forgiven him, either in this world
or in the next.' To deny the Son of Man is to reject Christ as
he is known to weak and fallible men often in a distorted
and unworthy form, and this no doubt is the sin of the
majority of people at the present day. It is a sin, in so far as it
is possible to know Christ better, though the degree of guilt
varies infinitely, but it is a sin that can be forgiven, because it
is often due to ignorance rather than to malice. But to sin
against the Holy Spirit is to reject the voice of God in the
conscience; it is to sin against the light which is given to
every man, by which alone he can come to know God, and if
a man sins against this light there is nothing which can save
him. 'If the light which is within you is darkness, how great
is the darkness.'

There is one other argument which can be used to support
this argument from scripture about the salvation of the 'unbeliever'. We know that when God assumed a human nature, he assumed the nature of all men and died for all men
without exception. There is therefore no one from the first
man to the last man who is excluded from the grace of Christ.
Though the manner in which this grace is extended may be
obscure to us, yet we cannot doubt its reality. It is helpful

perhaps to consider that in God's sight all men are in a sense one man. There is a 'mystical body' of humanity, which fell in Adam and was redeemed in Christ. It is as members of this body that men are saved, whatever may be the means by which grace reaches them and provided that they do not deliberately reject that grace.

17. Meeting at Rajpur

IN APRIL 1962 a meeting took place in Rajpur at the foot of the Himalayas of a group of Christians, Catholic and Protestant, to discuss the christian approach to Hinduism. The meeting took place at the invitation of Dr Cuttat, author of *The Encounter of Religions*, formerly lecturer in Comparative Religion at the Ecole des Hautes Etudes in Paris and Swiss Ambassador in New Delhi. It was the successor to a similar meeting which had taken place the previous year at Almora and at both meetings the purpose was not to have an academic discussion but rather a sharing of personal experience. The aim was to confront the Hindu and the christian experience of God, to try to enter deeply into both, to distinguish their differences and to relate them to one another. Hinduism is a religion which is based on experience, a unique experience of God, which was attained by the rishis in former times, was transmitted through the Vedas, especially the Upanishads, and later the Bhagavad Gita, has been developed with wonderful resourcefulness through Yoga and the Vedanta for more than two thousand years, and remains the living basis of religion to multitudes of Hindus at the present time.

This experience of God constitutes a tremendous challenge to the Christian. To many Hindus it appears as the ultimate experience of God, the supreme wisdom, which is India's gift to the world. It is for him the culmination of all religion, the ultimate truth to which all religion, christian included, must ultimately lead. Too often the Christian has been content to oppose this experience simply with the

dogma of his faith; to declare that the knowledge of God,
which is given in Christ, is the ultimate truth of religion, the
one thing necessary without which there can be no salvation.
This not unnaturally produces a strong reaction among
Hindus. The Christian is accused of being 'dogmatic' and
'intolerant' and of refusing to bring his religion to the test of
experience. It is the great merit of Dr Cuttat's book on *The
Encounter of Religions* that it has squarely met this challenge
by placing the meeting place of the two religions precisely
at this point of the experience of God. The purpose of our
meeting was to follow up the path which Dr Cuttat has
opened, to confront the two religions not in opposition
from without, but from within at the point where they meet
in the experience of God. This is obviously a far more difficult approach. It means entering into the other religion as
far as one is able to encounter it in depth and to relate it in a
living synthesis with one's own experience of faith. This is
no easy task, yet it would seem that this is just what is required of the Christian in India today. It may be mentioned
that both these meetings were held at American Protestant
houses, the present one at the Christian Study Centre at
Rajpur, and one of the most notable effects of this attempt to
confront the Hindu religious experience was to bring Catholics and Protestants together, each being engaged in facing
Hinduism in the light of his own living experience of
Christ.

   In order to give a more definite character to our discus-
sions we decided to take each day a representative example
of Hindu and christian spirituality, taking as representatives of Hinduism, Sankara, Ramana Maharshi, the Bhagavad Gita and Aurobindo, and of Christianity, Eckhart,
hesychasm, Gregory of Nyssa, and Teresa and John of
the Cross. In the opening discussion, Dr Cuttat indicated
the main lines which this confrontation should take. He
pointed out that the great stumbling-block for the Hindu

is the *fact of Christ*, the reality of the person, who 'suffered under Pontius Pilate'. Hinduism is a religion of total interiority and it has no place for historical fact. For a Christian, on the contrary, religion is a confrontation with an absolute Thou; it is the experience of a God who is made known objectively in the person of Christ and involves therefore *personal relationship*. But this does not mean that christian experience stops with the external; if it did there could be no dialogue with Hinduism. But in reality, for the Christian, the God who is absolutely other is also the God who is nearer than one's own self; the Christ who lived and suffered and died and rose again is also present in the inmost depths of the soul. Hindu interiority is, therefore, a challenge to us to meet Christ in this inmost depth of our being.

But there is a profound difference between Hindu and christian interiority. For the Hindu, interiority consists in a progressive detachment from everything both external and internal, leading to the isolation of the soul in its pure interiority. But for a Christian, interiority begins with repentance; it is the discovery of the abyss which separates the soul from God. But with this discovery goes the discovery of the love which bridges this abyss. Thus the soul in the interior abyss of its own being confronts God in the abyss of his being. It does not cut the connection with the unconscious, as is the purpose of Yoga, but opens the unconscious to the forgiveness of God, and from this experience of forgiveness the whole being is renewed; body and soul, *animus* and *anima*, are brought into unity with themselves and into communion with God. In the course of discussion it was suggested that it is this encounter with God as a person in the act of his love and forgiveness, which leads to the full realization of the human person, as a unique being, body, soul and spirit, made for communion with God. It was felt that in this mystery of the person, both in God and in man,

the distinctive character of the christian experience could
best be seen.

Sankara

Our first talk was on Sankara. It is in his doctrine and in his
interpretation of the mystical experience which underlies
Hindu religion, that we can see Hinduism in its purest form,
and though his doctrine was to be modified and opposed by
others, yet it remains basic in Hindu thought and brings us
nearest to the fundamental significance of Hinduism. It must
be remembered that Sankara based his whole doctrine on
sruti, that is on the revelation of the Vedas, and claimed to be
simply interpreting that doctrine, like a true theologian, in
the light of reason. He held that the ultimate truth cannot be
known either by sense or reason, but only by revelation. The
function of reason is simply to lead the soul, by means of
negation and analogy (*laksana*), to the experience of this ultimate reality which *sruti* reveals, in which both sense and
reason are transcended and the soul remains in a state of pure
consciousness, of simple awareness, in which no object is
'superimposed'. This state of consciousness is described
as 'without duality' (*advaita*); it is an experience of Being
'without a second'. Acording to Sankara this consciousness
always exists; it is eternal and unchanging, but objects are
'superimposed' on it through 'ignorance' (*avidya*) and the
soul is not aware of it. Wisdom (*vidya*) therefore is not
something which has to be acquired; it is something which
always exists and has to be 'discovered' or 'unveiled'. It is
this experience of the Self (*Atman*), in pure consciousness
'without duality', that constitutes the essence of the Hindu
mystical experience and which to the Hindu is both the ultimate truth and the ultimate reality. Other experiences of
God as a person, as an object of worship and devotion,
though not without value as a preparation for this, are

regarded as secondary. Ultimately all duality between God and man, as between man and all other beings, must be transcended and Being must be 'realized' in non-duality.

Such is the doctrine which Sankara expounds with remorseless logic in all his works. It should be noted, however, that it is not strictly correct to call this ultimate reality 'impersonal'. While maintaining that it cannot properly be defined, Sankara yet holds that it can best be described as 'being-knowledge-bliss' (*sacchidananda*) and this, clearly, should imply personality in some sense. At the same time it should be said that Sankara, when he describes the world as *maya*, does not mean that it has no being at all. He describes it as 'neither being nor not-being'. What he was principally concerned to do was to deny that the world has the same kind of being as the Brahman, that is absolute being. The world has relative being; it may even be said to have being 'by participation', or at least that is what his thought seems to imply. Yet the fact remains that ultimately, in the supreme knowledge (*paravidya*), there is no relation left between the world and God. In Advaita there is no place for any relation of any sort, the world and the soul are lost in God. This is where Hindu experience seems most clearly to go counter to christian experience. The relation of persons is transcended and since person necessarily implies relationship, this means that God is ultimately not a person at all.

Yet it is obvious that there is a profound truth underlying Sankara's conception of Advaita, a truth of experience, which has been continuously renewed throughout Indian history, and in Eckhart we find something which is extraordinarily like a form of christian Advaita. Eckhart is, of course, a controversial figure. He is often used by Hindus to prove that Christianity and Hinduism are ultimately identical in their doctrine. In his own lifetime he was condemned as a heretic, but he certainly believed himself to be orthodox and modern Catholic scholarship tends to support him. His

doctrine is certainly of extraordinary interest. His basic
principle is that the intellect (*Vernunft*) in man transcends
time and space and multiplicity and makes man 'like God'.
The intellect goes beyond not only the world of the senses
but beyond every conception. 'Intellect is not satisfied with
goodness or with wisdom or with truth – or even with God
himself . . . It does not rest but breaks through to the bottom
from which emerge goodness and truth . . . It goes through
to the root from which springs the Son and the Holy
Ghost.' Eckhart maintains that in order to reach this goal
the soul must be detached from all forms whatever, even
from the sacraments, the saints, the angels and our Lady. It
must go beyond 'God' in order to reach the 'Godhead'. No
one will question the radical nature of this doctrine, and on
the surface it certainly looks heretical. Eckhart appears to
go, like Sankara, beyond all forms of thought and relationship whether of reason or revelation, beyond even the distinctions in the trinity, to the 'naked being' of God.

Yet we must remember that Eckhart was building on the
christian doctrine of grace. This ascent to God takes place
for him 'in Christ', that is in the Word, and what he seems
to be seeking is the participation of the intellect in God's own
knowledge of himself. Now it is strictly true to say that in
God's own knowledge of himself in his Word there are no
real distinctions. God knows himself and all created things
in one simple pure act of knowledge, which is identical with
his being. In this sense it is true to say that the knowledge
of God is '*advaita*', without duality. As Aquinas teaches,
'ideas' in God, that is God's knowledge of created things,
are identical with the divine essence. If therefore the soul
by grace should participate in God's own mode of knowledge
it would know all things, itself included, in this simple
mode of knowledge 'without duality'. This seems to be
what Eckhart really intended to say, and one may suggest
that this is the underlying truth contained in the doctrine of

Sankara. Yet it remains true that, though 'identified' with
God by knowledge, the soul yet remains distinct by nature.
Though the mode of knowledge is different and distinctions, *as we conceive them*, cease to exist, yet the distinctions
remain in reality. Man and the world are not lost in God,
nor are the persons absorbed in the unity of the Godhead. It
is these distinctions which christian orthodoxy is concerned
to maintain, since they allow for relationship both between
man and man in the mystical body of Christ, and between
man and God. They leave a 'space' for the relation of love
between persons, between the person of God and his creatures and between the persons within the Godhead. It is
probable that Eckhart intended to retain these distinctions
but his language often obscures them. Yet perhaps more
than anyone else he shows the deep underlying truth of the
doctrine of Advaita, and helps us to see that it is only in the
christian doctrines of the trinity and the incarnation that the
mystery of love and personal relationship in God and man
can be reconciled with the absolute unity and simplicity of
the Godhead, and its absolute transcendence.

Ramana Maharshi

Perhaps the most remarkable example of advaitic experience
in modern times is that of Ramana Maharshi. His story is well
known. While still a boy at school, he believed that he was
about to die and underwent in imagination the experience of
death, surrendering himself totally to it. This brought about
a kind of mystical death in his soul. From that moment he
entered into advaitic consciousness, which remained with
him till the end of his life. His experience is all the more remarkable because he knew nothing of advaitic doctrine at
this time; it was only afterwards that he found his own personal experience explained and confirmed in the doctrine
of Advaita. There is no doubt that his was an experience of

extraordinary psychological depth; it brought about a complete transformation in his life. And yet, though at first he was subject to trances and lived almost without food or sleep, yet in the course of time he came to live a normal life enjoying the pure consciousness of *advaita* and yet able to act in everyday life with understanding and humility, humour and charity. He is an example of the *jivanmukti*, the soul which is 'delivered' once for all, according to the Hindu view, and yet continues to live on in this world.

Ramana Maharshi is an example of Hindu mystical experience which is of extraordinary interest, both because he is almost contemporary (he died in 1951) and because he reveals the ideal of Advaita in its purest form. What are we to say of this experience? It seems that we must admit in the first place that it is an authentic mystical experience, that is, an experience of the Absolute. It is generally explained (as by Maritain, for instance) that the soul, passing beyond all the experience of the senses and of reason, experiences itself in its own substantial being, in its own *esse*. It knows itself in a simple act of reflection without image or concept, and in this experience of the self, it experiences indirectly the presence of God, the absolute Being. Using Ramana's own terms, one may say that passing beyond the temporal, phenomenal self, the empirical 'I', the soul reaches the ground of the Self, the absolute 'I'. It becomes aware of the eternal 'I am', which is the ground not only of its own being but of all being. This would be the highest experience open to man in the natural order. The soul realizes at once its own nothingness (apart from God) and the infinite being of God as the source and the support and the end of its own and all other being.

One may say that this is typical of all mystical experience. Something akin to it is found in Buddhism, in Taoism, in islamic mysticism and in Plotinus. It is to be found also in christian mysticism at least in some degree, from Evagrius and Dionysius to Eckhart, Ruysbroeck and John of the Cross. In all alike there is to be found an experience, which goes beyond all distinctions of sense and reason, and encounters absolute Being 'without duality'; in all alike it is an experience which brings with it supreme conviction and supreme bliss. But though this experience certainly enters into Christianity, the Christian is always concerned to uphold those distinctions of which not only reason but also faith assure him. Indeed one may say that it is precisely our christian faith which assures us of the reality of these distinctions between man and God and between created things. It is because we believe in Christ, God and man, mediating between God and the world, that we maintain that these distinctions remain even in the highest mystical experience. In the experience of God as the ultimate 'I am', the soul experiences itself as called into being by God, as a 'word' uttered by God, analogous to his eternal utterance of the divine Word. But may we not say that this experience is in a sense 'without duality'? There is here no distinction of subject and object as Sankara conceived them, no 'superimposition' of anything on the absolute. The soul knows itself in a personal relationship to God, a relation of knowledge and love, which implies no separation. There is a presence of one to the other, a mutual indwelling, in which the soul knows with God's own knowledge and loves with God's own love, and yet remains distinct in nature; much as in the trinity, while the persons remain eternally distinct in their personal relationship, yet there is a mutual indwelling, in which they are absolutely one, 'without duality', sharing the same nature, the same pure act of being, knowledge and love.

It is the hesychast doctrine of the Orthodox Church with its teaching on the Prayer of the Heart that we can find this distinctive character of christian mysticism most clearly revealed. This doctrine was fully developed only in the eleventh century, but it is supposed to go back to the monks of Mount Sinai in the fifth century. Its most important concept is that of the 'heart' as the root or ground of the personality, pre-conceptual, pre-affective and pre-voluntary. The heart is the centre of the being, where God dwells and the whole effort of prayer is directed towards finding the 'place of the heart'. It is obvious that we have here a point of meeting with the Advaita doctrine, yet at the same time the distinctive character of the christian experience comes out very clearly. Once the soul has entered into this interior depth, it discovers the uncreated light, shining in the darkness, and immediately it realizes its own nothingness and sin, and its first movement is a cry for mercy, a movement of repentance. It is precisely in this interior depth that, according to the Fathers, the 'war with the demons' begins. Thus the christian experience begins with repentance, with the acknowledgement of sin and the abyss which separates the soul from God. But with it goes the experience of God's grace and mercy, of the divine descent, which bridges the gulf. It is an experience of the in-dwelling of the Holy Spirit, which separates from sin and leads to contemplation (*theoria*), the experience of God himself.

The Orthodox doctrine of contemplation has a well-defined character. It begins with the contemplation of the divine 'energies' in nature. Behind all the outward forms of nature the eastern Fathers believed that there were the divine energies (also called *logoi* and akin to the platonic ideas), which sustain them in their being, and it is the work of the mystic to penetrate behind the outward forms to these divine energies, so that he becomes, as it were, assimilated to the rhythms of the universe, which he then offers up to God, thus acting as the high-priest of nature. The resemblance of this doctrine to certain forms of Yoga is obvious and is surely instructive. The next stage of contemplation is the contemplation of the divine mysteries in the scriptures where, passing beyond God's revelation of himself in nature, the soul contemplates his revelation of himself in Christ and in the whole mystery of Christ, revealed in the Old and the New Testament. But the final stage is a contemplation of God in himself, that is in the trinity. In this experience it is said that the soul knows God through his image in itself, so that the soul in knowing itself knows God whose image it is. There is clearly a profound analogy here with the experience of *advaita*, but with this important difference, that here the image of God in the soul is not merely the natural image, which is derived from creation, but the supernatural image which is formed by the indwelling of the trinity in the soul. Perhaps here we come as close as we can to the analogy and at the same time the difference of the Hindu and the christian experience of God.

The Bhagavad Gita

Within the Hindu tradition the Bhagavad Gita represents the point at which the devotion to a personal God, derived from the school of the Bhagavatas, the worshippers of the 'Lord' (*Bhagavan*), is brought into direct relation with the conception of the absolute Brahman. It cannot be denied that in Gita the Hindu genius rises to a wonderful conception of the absolute as a personal God. Krishna is here identified with the supreme Brahman, the *para-brahman* who is also the *paramatman*, the supreme Self, and the way to union with God is held to be not merely the way of 'knowledge' (*jnana*) but the way of total surrender in love (*bhakti*). When we consider that Krishna is at the same time an *avatara*, a 'descent' of God, by which the eternal is manifested in time, it is clear how close Hindu thought comes at this point to Christianity. Yet one may say that Hindu thought never achieves a fully convincing idea either of a personal God or of an incarnation. Sankara also believed in the personal God of the Gita, but for him the personal God, in so far as he manifests God's relation to man, belongs to the world of *maya*. In the absolute Brahman, the personal God, like every other form of 'superimposition' on the absolute, disappears. He is a guide on the path to the absolute, but ultimately both he and his disciple must disappear in the Brahman. Ramanuja tried to safeguard the personal God and to make him truly absolute, but in doing so he was led to allow of 'modes' and 'attributes' in the Brahman, giving him a personal form and a personal body and thus destroying the simplicity of the Godhead, which Sankara was determined to defend at all costs. Yet the Gita, and the whole tradition of Vaishnavism with its devotion to a personal God, is surely a living witness to the need which the Indian soul has always felt for a God who is a person, an object of worship and love, who can make himself known in a human form and manifest his love to his disciples.

The other theme which dominates the Bhagavad Gita is that of 'action' as opposed to knowledge. In the Upanishads the way to union with God has been conceived as the way of knowledge; to know the Brahman was to become one with the Brahman, or rather it was to recognize the identity of the Atman with the Brahman which always exists. The result was that union with God was held to belong only to those who could attain to this higher wisdom, which in practice meant the yogis and ascetics, who could undertake the discipline of mind and body which was necessary for this. The message of the Gita was that union with God was open also to the householder living in the world. Action (*karma*) which was done not for personal gain but in a spirit of detachment, seeking not the 'fruit of action' but offering it as a sacrifice to God, was shown to be a way of union no less valid than the way of knowledge. This again is related to the idea of a personal God. 'If I did no work,' Krishna declares, 'these worlds would perish.' It is the action of God which

sustains the world and yet this action of God is without
attachment. It produces no change in the divine nature:
'actions do not taint me,' says Krishna, 'nor have I any
thirst for the result of action. He who knows me thus is not
fettered by action.' Thus the divine action is a model for
human action. It would seem that the Hindu mind was moving here to a conception of God not simply as the ultimate
'I am', but as the absolute in action; to an idea that the world
is not simply *maya* but the effect of the divine action, and that
man is called to co-operate in this divine action. Yet again
Hinduism finds it difficult to sustain this insight. Ultimately it is driven to hold that the world is not real; there
is no real creation and therefore no real incarnation. There
can be no redemptive action in history leading the world to
its consummation through time, because ultimately time and
history are not real. The only deliverance is ultimately the
deliverance from time itself into the timeless reality.

Nevertheless it is in the Bhagavad Gita that we feel above
all the richness and depth of Hindu religion and its close-
ness to Christianity. If, as Father Johanns maintained, we
introduce the idea of creation, so that the world is given a
reality, not of course of the same nature as the reality of God
but analogous to it, a relative reality wholly derived from the
being of God, then Hindu doctrine becomes 'open' to Christ.
We can then begin to conceive of a christian theology which
would be built upon the doctrine of the Vedanta as it was
once built on the doctrine of Plato and Aristotle.

If we want an example of the method of the Fathers in this
respect, we cannot find a better model than Gregory of
Nyssa, the brother of Basil and friend of Gregory of
Nazianzus. Here we find a christian philosopher, whose
brothers and sisters and father and mother and grandmother
were canonized saints, who yet after a pious education at home
deliberately goes to a pagan university to study Greek
philosophy and to bring it into 'captivity' to Christ. The

philosophy which Gregory studied was that of Plotinus, the
neo-platonist, whose doctrine is nearer to that of the Vedanta than any other system in the West. It is therefore of peculiar interest to us. Gregory follows Plato and Plotinus
step by step in the path of the spiritual life. For him as for
them it is a process of separation from the material world, of
gradual purification from the passions leading to *apatheia*,
of the return from multiplicity to unity, from the exterior to
the interior, from appearance to reality. Essentially, and it is
here that we can see most clearly its affinity with Hindu
doctrine, it is a return to the self, to the true self, the *nous*
which is the image of God. For Gregory, as for Plotinus,
the knowledge of God is found in the knowledge of the self.
Yet it is here precisely that we find the fundamental difference between the two systems. For Plotinus the *nous* is by
nature divine; to know oneself is to know one's divine nature, which has been obscured through the turning of the
mind to the world of the senses. But for Gregory the *nous*
is not divine by nature; it is the 'image' of God; it is a created
likeness of God; and what the soul discovers when it returns to itself is the divine life, the *pneuma,* which is not its
own being but a gift of God, a communication of God, which
is reflected in the soul.

Here again we find the fundamental difference between
christian mysticism and every form of natural mysticism.
For the natural mystic, whether Plotinus or Sankara, the soul
is by nature divine; to know God is to discover one's own
nature, to recognize the divinity within, which has been
hidden by ignorance. But for the Christian the soul is an image
of God, a created likeness of God, in which God dwells by
grace, by the free gift of himself to the soul. To know oneself is to know oneself as the image of God, to 'participate in
the divine nature', to know God with God's own knowledge
of himself; but it is also to receive this knowledge as a gift of
God, to be united by a love which unites two distinct na-

tures in an eternal relation of love. This knowledge and love are surely 'without duality'; there is no relation of subject and object, but an 'I-Thou' relationship, which makes two persons one in distinction of nature but in unity of mind and will. It is important also to observe that for St Gregory the image of God in man is not merely individual but social. Ultimately it is 'mankind' which is the image of God, and the perfect image of God is found in Christ who unites all mankind in one body in himself. Thus the soul is not isolated in its union with God, but on the contrary joined to all men in that ultimate ground of their nature where all are one. So also man is not separated from nature; man forms part of the whole creation and 'in Christ' the whole creation returns to God. Thus for the Christian there is a real world, a real progress in time, a real redemption by which the fallen world is restored to unity in Christ; and this unity is nothing else but the participation of man, and through man of all nature, in the very being of God, sharing by grace in God's own mode of being, knowledge and bliss.

Sri Aurobindo

Thus we can see how christian experience, because of its belief in the reality of the world, of time and history, of nature and person, distinguishes itself from Hindu experience; and yet how, once this is granted, it should be able to integrate the Hindu experience in itself, thus leading it to the goal which it seems to have been seeking. We can see a remarkable example of the movement of Hindu thought to achieve this kind of integration in itself in the work of Aurobindo. His example is the more interesting in that he was brought up entirely by western standards and educated in the West. It was only on his return to India after completing his education that he made the discovery of Hinduism. This came to him during the time of his imprisonment under the

British, when he had a vision of Krishna in which he believed that he received the charge to restore Hinduism to its true place in the life of the Indian people. The rest of his life in his ashram at Pondicherry, until his death in 1950, was spent in the attempt to fulfil this mission.

But it was not for nothing that Aurobindo had been educated in the West. His philosophy is in reality a remarkable development of the tradition of the Vedanta in the light of western, and implicitly christian, thought. For Aurobindo the world of becoming is not unreal. It is a self-manifestation of the eternal. There is not only a movement of ascent of the world to God, but also a movement of descent of God into the world, and the mediator between these two movements is the supermind. It is the supermind which enables the absolute to manifest itself in space and time, and the world of space and time to 'return' to God. What is of particular interest is that Aurobindo conceives this process of return not as a negation of the world of becoming, but as its fulfilment. Spiritual consciousness in his system does not abolish the universe, it takes it up and transforms it, restoring it to its ground in the divine mind. This is the process of what Aurobindo calls 'integral Yoga'. We have surely here a remarkable example of the convergence of Hindu and christian thought.

Yet one may question whether Aurobindo with his concept of the supermind is able to solve the essential problem of the Vedanta. For he also has no clear concept of creation. For the Vedanta the problem always arises that if the world is conceived to be real, it is never adequately distinguished from God, so that it falls into pantheism, that is to say, the world is considered to be divine; or if, like Sankara, it is determined to preserve the purity of the divine nature, then it is compelled to deny the reality of the world. An interesting comparison was suggested between Sankara and Ramanuja, on the one hand, and John of the Cross and Teresa, on the other. Abbot Chapman confessed that at one time he looked upon John of the Cross as a 'Buddhist'. There is no doubt that John of the Cross carried the way of negation, in the manner of Buddhism, as far as it can go. His method was that of total abnegation, both active and passive, of the senses and the understanding, that is, a total denial of the self, leading to a union with God beyond sense and reason. But it must be noted that in John of the Cross, the mode of the senses and the understanding is transcended only that their term may be reached. Ultimately the whole world is recovered with the plenitude of its being in God. Instead of God being known through the world, through the operation of the senses and the understanding, it is the world which is known through God, that is, through the divine mode of knowledge.

May we not say that it was towards this vision of the world in God that Sankara, and with him the whole tradition of Advaita, was being led, but that the terms of his philosophy were not adequate to enable him to reach the goal? We must never forget that in the Brahman of the Upanishads there is an absolute plenitude of being; the Brahman is *purnam* and to it nothing can be added. When the world is added to the Brahman it does not make it more, and when it is taken away it does not make it less. In Sankara this is explained by the doctrine that the world has no real being distinct from the being of Brahman; its real being is the being of the Brahman and all appearance of difference is an illusion. It is so also with the self. The Atman is the Brahman, that is the essential message of Advaita; there is no real distinction between the soul and God.

Ramanuja

Ramanuja too held that the Atman and the Brahman are one, but he was determined to maintain a distinction between

God and man. His position may be compared to that of
Teresa. He was not primarily a philosopher but a devotee.
He belonged to the school of the Bhagavatas, the worshippers of Vishnu, who were devotees of a personal God, and
his purpose was to guide these devotees on the path of the
love of God like a St Teresa. There is no doubt that Ramanuja sought to avoid pantheism. He believed in the utter transcendence of God (Isvara.) Yet in order to preserve a distinction between God and the soul, and so to leave a place for
the worship and the love of God, he was led to conceive of
the soul as a 'mode' or 'attribute' (*prakara*) of Isvara. He
could even speak of the soul as a 'part' (*amsa*) of the Brahman, or as the body of which Isvara is the soul. His philosophical defence of this view was the rather curious idea that
as a substance may have many attributes – the lotus for instance, may be red or white or blue – but the substance itself
remains unchanged, so Isvara having an infinite number of
'auspicious' attributes remains itself unchanged. Whatever
the defects of his philosophy, however, it is clear that
Ramanuja was moved above all by the love of God and the
desire to bring souls to the knowledge and the love of God,
that is, the intuition of the 'highest Self', which is the 'essential attribute' of the soul. When we add that in Ramanuja's
doctrine divine grace (*prasada*) is an essential element in the
return of the soul to God, and that it is in his *avataras*, his
'descents' to save the world, that Vishnu makes himself
known to his worshippers, once again we cannot but be impressed by the 'christian' sense of the Hindu soul, *anima
naturaliter christiana*, if ever there was one. In this light the
whole of the Vedanta seems a long preparation of the Indian
soul for the coming of Christ. All the material is there, waiting only for the Word to be spoken, that it may come to new
life and be built up into a living synthesis of christian doctrine.

At the conclusion of our meeting the thought that re-

mained most strongly with us all was that our task in India
is not so much to bring Christ to India (as though he could
be absent), as to discover Christ already present and active
in the Hindu soul. After all these centuries of preparation,
Christ awaits his birth in the Hindu soul. It is for us to recognize his presence, to enter with deep sympathy into the
movement of Hindu thought and experience which is leading it to Christ; to make contact with the Hindu in that inner
depth of his being where he has so constantly sought God,
and there to act as midwife, in the manner of Socrates, to the
birth of Christ. But if we are to do this it needs great love and
humility as well as serious thought and study on our part.

18. The Unknown Christ of Hinduism

IN A RECENT book, *The Unknown Christ of Hinduism* (London, 1965), Dr Raymond Panikkar, who himself comes from a Hindu family on one side and a Catholic family on the other, has suggested a new approach. Like Dr Cuttat, he recognizes that the meeting of religions cannot take place in the sphere of 'natural reason' or in any abstract sphere of comparative religion. It has to be an existential encounter, a meeting of persons who are fully committed to religious faith. But whereas Cuttat had suggested that each party in this encounter must take what Husserl called an *epoche*, a kind of placing in brackets of his own particular faith so as to meet in the common ground of the 'holy', Raymond Panikkar boldly says that the meeting must take place 'in Christ'. From a christian point of view, when its full implications are understood, this seems to me to be the most profound approach that can be made. Whether it can ever be acceptable to a Hindu, a Buddhist or a Muslim is another matter, yet I feel that the attempt has to be made. It certainly demands great humility on the part of the Christian and a considerable deepening of his faith, but it places the whole problem at the deepest theological level, and enables us to see the full implications of the christian faith.

We have to begin from the fact that according to Paul the whole creation takes place 'in Christ', 'In him all created things took their being . . . they were all created in him and through him and for him . . . and in him all subsist' (Col 1: 16–17). The whole creation is a 'theophany', a manifestation of God; but this manifestation takes place in Christ, and thus the whole creation becomes a 'christophany', a manifestation of Christ. The Father manifests himself in his Son or Word, who by taking our human flesh assumes the whole creation to himself and fills it with his presence (Eph 4: 10). We cannot properly speaking think of anything apart from Christ; it is he who gives existence its meaning. At the same time Christ is also the redeemer of the world. When he took our human flesh, he took the flesh of all mankind and redeemed our human nature. There is therefore no one from the beginning to the end of the world, who is not redeemed by Christ. It is in the light of this conception of Christ as the creator and redeemer and we must add the sanctifier of the world, who communicates to man his Spirit and makes him partake of the divine nature, that we must see the whole problem of the religion (rather than the religions) of the world.

The idea of a universal or 'cosmic' revelation which preceded all special forms of revelation, is basic to the biblical view of religion and is found in all christian tradition. In the biblical view all men were originally included in God's plan of salvation. In the New Testament, John speaks of the Word which 'enlightens every man who comes into the world'. St Justin took up this view among the Fathers and spoke of the Word or Logos having been revealed 'in part' to the Greeks and other peoples, and 'fully' in Christ (Ap. I, 46, 1-3; II, 10, 1-3). Clement of Alexandria spoke of Greek philosophy as being a 'pedagogue' to lead men to Christ like the Law to the Jews (Str. VI, 5, 42). Origen in his turn taking up a theme of the early Fathers spoke of the Church as 'existing in all the saints who lived since the beginning of time' (Comm, Song of Songs, II, 8), and Augustine in a well known passage declared that the christian religion had existed 'from the beginning; though it had only come to be known as such from the time of Christ' (Retr., I, 12).

Thus there is a solid tradition according to which Christianity, that is to say the mystery of Christ and the Church,
can be said to have existed from the beginning of the world.
It is present in creation, because the whole creation finds its
meaning and its purpose in Christ, who assumes the whole
material universe into the life of God. It is present in all history, because Christ comes as the 'fulfilment' of history and
reveals the nature of human destiny. Above all, it is found in
the different religious traditions of the world, because in
them this 'mystery' is gradually unfolded. If Clement of
Alexandria could find in Greek philosophy a 'preparation'
for Christ like the Law for the Jews, how much more can we
find it in Hinduism, Buddhism, Taoism and Islam. In the
Hindu conception of the Atman, the true Self of every man,
who is one with the Brahman, the ultimate Reality; in the
Buddhist conception of the Buddha – nature existing in all
men; in the Taoist conception of the Tao as existing before
all things and containing the meaning of all things; in the
Muslim Sufi's conception of the Qutb, the 'pole' of the universe, who is also the Perfect Man; we have so many 'prophecies' as it were of the mystery of Christ.

From a christian point of view there is therefore no difficulty
in seeing in Christ the fulfilment of all religion. We can say
that the mystery of Christ is 'hidden' in all religion as it was
hidden in Judaism, and that Christ himself comes to reveal
this hidden meaning, to make clear what was obscure, to
make explicit what was implicit, to perfect what was imperfect. At the same time we have to say that in this process
every religion has to undergo a kind of death. Just as Judaism had to die that it might be born again in Christ, so also
with every other religion. There had to be a death and a resurrection, a death to all that is imperfect and temporal, which
may be exceedingly painful, as human feelings are so deeply
involved in these temporal aspects of religion; but at the

same time a resurrection in which all that is essential, the eternal reality underlying the temporal forms, is preserved.

From a christian point of view, as has been said, there can be no objection to this. But what of the point of view of other religions? Can they be expected to accept this role of being 'preparations', of having no finality? On the surface this is a grave difficulty and is likely to meet with violent opposition. Yet if we can get beneath the surface, it may not prove so unacceptable. In the first place, we must recognize that all religions are in a state of continual evolution. It is illusory to regard them as so many fixed forms. Hinduism today with its temple worship and its different forms of devotion is immeasurably remote from the early religion of the Vedas; Mahayana Buddhism with its conception of the Bodhisattva, who refuses to enter Nirvana until the whole world has been saved, is no less remote from the early Hinayana Buddhism; the mysticism of the great Sufis, even of one so orthodox as Al Ghazali, is an extraordinary development of the primitive faith of Islam. So also, we must admit, is the traditional Christianity, whether of Catholicism or of Orthodoxy, with its development of worship and theology and canon law, a very different thing from the primitive judaic Christianity of the early Church.

Thus all religion is in a state of continuous development, and in this process it is undergoing influence from outside. We may believe that in each religion there is a vital principle, an inner law, which enables it to assimilate elements from outside while preserving its intrinsic character, but the evolution cannot be questioned. There is therefore no reason why we should not envisage a 'meeting' of religions today, in which each will grow by contact with the others. A Christian will believe that in this process of growth the christian faith will always retain its essential character; it will never renounce anything of the truth which it has received. But the

demands made upon it may be no less exacting than those on
other religions. We may believe that Christianity will be
called upon to renounce its western forms of thought and
behaviour, which may be as painful a renunciation as anything required of the Buddhist or the Hindu in the encounter
with Christ. The forms of worship and of theology and of
canon law which have grown up in the Church in Europe
were derived from Syrian, Greek and Roman traditions, and
are all 'accidental' elements in Christianity. To adopt the
forms of India or China or Africa would lead to a radical
transformation of the outward expression of the christian
faith, even though nothing were changed of its essential
truth.

Thus Christianity no less than the other religions of the
world is required to undergo a death and resurrection, if it is
to enter into a genuine dialogue with other religious traditions and become adapted to Asia and Africa. On the other
hand, these other traditions, though they also may be called
to renounce much of their outward form, will not be untrue
to themselves. If our argument is correct, if there is a genuine presence of the mystery of Christ in every religion, then
for that religion to find Christ is not to renounce its own
truth, but on the contrary to discover it. It is to find the hidden meaning of its own doctrine through all the stages of
its evolution; it is to enter into the interior depth of the
meaning of its scriptures and to find their ultimate meaning,
just as to find Christ in the Old Testament is to discover its
authentic meaning.

This shows us the ultimate nature of this 'meeting' of religions. It is a movement of 'return to the sources', of redis-
covering the interior depth of each religious tradition, such
as is now taking place in the Catholic as well as in other religions. But this movement has to take place not in isolation,
but in a profound encounter with all that is most fundamental in each religious tradition. As we come to the inner depth

of our own tradition, we find ourselves drawing near to the depths of the other traditions, and it is in that interior depth that the final meeting has to take place. A Christian will believe that in this interior depth every man will encounter Christ, because it is the mystery of Christ which lies at the heart of all religion. But he has not to impose his belief on others; he has only to join with them in that search for the ultimate truth and to allow Christ to reveal himself in his own way to all those who seek the truth in charity.

PART FIVE

Conclusion

19. The Renewal of the Church

THERE ARE three movements which have steadily grown in strength within the Church during the last fifteen or twenty years: the biblical movement, the liturgical movement and the ecumenical movement. Each of these movements grew up separately and has its own special history, but we can now begin to see how close a bearing each has upon the others. The close relation of the biblical movement to the liturgical movement has been recognized, in fact, for some time, because the liturgy has its roots in the bible and there can be no intelligent grasp of the liturgy apart from the bible. But the relation of the bible and the liturgy to the ecumenical movement has not been so clearly seen. Yet it was on this very question of the place of the bible and the liturgy in the Church that the controversy originally started by the Reformation turned.

Even now one of the commonest charges made against Catholics by Protestants is that they do not know their bible, and it must be admitted that in many instances the charge is justified. The reasons for this go far back into history. There is no need to emphasize the pre-eminent place which the bible held in the life of the Christian in the early Church; it was the source alike of doctrine and of moral conduct. Yet many Protestants would now be willing to agree that the bible was never considered independently of the Church. The bible was regarded as the book of the Church. It was from the Church that the Christian received the bible; it was the Church which had to decide what books could be called canonical and could therefore be read in the

churches. At the same time it was in the liturgical assembly
that the scriptures were normally read and it was there
that they received their authentic commentary from those
who were authorized to preach in the Church's name.

From this arose the fact that the earliest theology of the
Church consisted largely of commentaries on the scriptures.
Some of the greatest works of the Fathers, like John
Chrysostom and Cyril of Alexandria, Ambrose and Augustine, are their commentaries on the bible, given originally
to the people in their liturgical assemblies. Even when these
commentaries were not given in public, it was through deep
meditation on the scriptures that theology developed. Right
up to the time of Aquinas the chief task of a *doctor* of the
Church was held to be the exposition of the bible so that
he could be called *magister sacrae paginae*, a 'master of the
sacred page'. The famous 'Sentences' of Peter Lombard, on
which the theologian was required to comment, were in
fact nothing but a string of scriptural texts arranged according to subjects.

It is worthwhile remarking also what an important place
the bible held in the life of a Benedictine monk in early
times. It has even been suggested that the sole reading of
most of the monk's of Benedict's time was the bible. Even
if this is an exaggeration, it remains true that their principal
reading was the bible, and the rest of their reading was
nearly all commentaries on the bible by such writers as
Jerome, Augustine and Gregory. But there is an important
difference in the character of the reading of the monk. The
monk did not read in order to speculate or develop a
theology. For him the bible was the rule of life as he had
been taught in the Rule of St Benedict: 'What page or what
utterance of the divinely inspired books of the Old and New
Testament is not an unerring rule of human life?' A modern
reader might be inclined to question the truth of this in
regard to the Old Testament, but no one will question the

value of this discipline of bible reading in the formation of character. It was this that gave its special character both to the life and to the thought of the monk. When he came to write, like Bede and Bernard, his writing, even if it was not actually a commentary of the bible, was inevitably couched in biblical terms. Recently, we have come to recognize how great was the value of this 'monastic theology', which was at once so biblical in its mode of thought and expression, and so firmly directed towards contemplation and charity, so that it was never lost in arid speculation.

The growth of scholastic theology inevitably changed all this. Though it was still based on the teaching of the scriptures, its mode of expression was no longer biblical and its mode of thought was determined by the principles of Aristotle rather than by those of the bible. The result was, of course, an immense gain in clarity of thought and systematic development, but it opened the way to a separation between theology and the life of prayer, and still more between the language of the 'schools' and the language of the ordinary man. The Church was suffering from this divorce at the Reformation, and it has continued to suffer till the present day.

For the bible, the liturgy, theology, and the life of prayer, which had before formed a closely interwoven unity, were divided into different compartments and each suffered alike. Theology went its own way, becoming ever more abstract and remote from ordinary habits of thought and language. The liturgy, based as it was on biblical modes of thought, became more and more alien to the new way of thinking and lost its importance in the life of prayer. Prayer, in consequence, began to develop its own rather artificial methods of meditation as a substitute for that patient meditation on the scriptures, which had been the way of the monks and of all christian antiquity.

.   .   .

We can now understand how it was that at the Reformation the bible held such a small place in the life of the christian people and how Luther could conceive that it was his great task to restore the bible to its proper place in the christian life. Thus Catholic piety tended to develop after the Reformation apart from the bible, through popular devotions like the rosary and the stations of the cross, and through popular books of piety like the *Imitation of Christ*, which, however devout in its own way, is very far from the spirituality of the gospels. Even now Catholic piety remains more or less fixed in this mould, and it is for this reason that the liturgical movement makes such slow progress. May it not be that this is also one reason why Catholics generally seem to be so lacking in a social sense, and that communism so often finds an easy entry into a Catholic country? The whole structure of this piety is individualistic and tends to turn the soul away from engagement in the world and in history.

The biblical and the liturgical movements must therefore be seen as a return to the sources of christian life, a renewal of the christian spirit in its depths, which will work a transformation in Catholic life, alike in theology, in prayer and in social life. The biblical view of life is essentially social and historical. The divine revelation was given not merely to individuals, but to a people, and in so far as it was given to individuals, it was given to them precisely as the representatives of their people. Nor was it given to people withdrawn from the world, but to a people involved in the most intense drama of history. The christian revelation is above all the revelation of God in history; it is this that sets it apart from all other religious systems in the world. The modern study of the bible aims above all at recovering this historical setting of divine revelation.

Scholastic theology, of course, makes abundant use of the bible, but it translates it all into its own mode of abstract thought. Biblical theology aims at recovering the original Hebrew mode of thought and expression and so restoring to the christian message its original shape. This is already beginning to have its influence on the teaching of christian doctrine, where the new German catechism has begun to serve as a model for a method of teaching which substitutes for the dry and abstract formulas of the old catechism the living language of the original gospel message.

It is here that we can see the essential relation of the biblical movement to the liturgy. The first part of the mass, the mass of the catechumens, is now coming to be recognized more clearly for what it is, that is as a form of catechesis. It is intended to be an instruction in the mysteries of the faith. The people assemble first of all to 'hear the word of God.' It is this that has given such urgency to the movement for the use of the vernacular in the mass. If the first part of the mass is an instruction, the first necessity is that it should be understood, and this means for the majority of people that it must be in their own language. The people must be able not only to hear but to understand the word of God.

This again brings back the sermon to its proper place within the liturgy. The purpose of the sermon is to interpret the word of God, to give that kind of commentary on the bible which the Fathers were accustomed to give, a custom which has left us such masterpieces of christian wisdom as Augustine's Commentaries on the Psalms and on St John's Gospel. So here again we see the need of a biblical theology. a theology which takes its departure from the word of God, itself, and interprets it along the lines of biblical thought. This means that the sermon will be engaged in history, not in the sense of politics so much as of seeing the history of the world in the light of God's revelation and showing the Christian his place in the scheme of things.

But the liturgy does not merely involve listening to

the word of God and its interpretation – it means taking an
active part. There is first of all the people's response to the
word, which is found in the songs of the Gradual and
Alleluia and the other chants. Here we can see how the
psalms can once again come to be the prayer of the christian
people. It would demand no doubt a restoration of the
psalms to their original length instead of the short extracts
which we now have. In this respect the Gélineau psalms have
shown how effective the psalms can be for community
singing. Thus the first part of the mass would become a
popular service in which the whole people joined in singing
praises to God in their own language and with appropriate
music. In many quarters it has also been suggested that the
litany, which now survives only on Good Friday, should be
restored at the end of the mass of the catechumens. This
again, being said in the vernacular and answering to the
needs of the parish and the people as a whole, could become
a really popular form of prayer.

But we should still be far from the ideal of restoring the
mass to its proper place in the life of the people, if we were
to stop with the first part of the mass. The mass is above all
a sacrifice, the sacrifice of the mystical body of Christ, and it
is in the sense of its full participation in this sacrifice that
the people can recover the full meaning of the mass in their
lives. Here again we need to go back to the biblical basis of
the mass to see how the christian people is that 'chosen
race, a royal priesthood, a consecrated nation,' of which St
Peter speaks, whose function is to 'be a holy priesthood to
offer up sacrifices to God through Jesus Christ'. There is no
need to emphasize here that this priesthood of the whole
people, which according to Aquinas is conferred in baptism,
in no way detracts from the unique character of the priesthood in those who are ordained as ministers for that special
purpose. The priest alone 'makes' the sacrifice, that is to say
makes the sacrifice of Christ really present, but the whole

people joins with him in offering it to God and thereby is formed into the mystical body of Christ and realizes its social character as the people of God, destined to carry out the work of Christ in the world.

Having described the character of the biblical and liturgical movements in these terms, there is no need to point out how close this brings us to our Protestant brethren and how important it is therefore for the ecumenical movement. Two of the principles for which the Protestants fought at the Reformation were that the bible should be in the hands of every Christian to be the guide and inspiration of his life, and that the worship of the christian people should be the common worship of the 'priestly people' in its own tongue. Both these principles can now be seen to be fully Catholic; it is simply going back to what was the normal custom of the Church in the early centuries. The fixation of the bible and the liturgy in Latin in the West was due to an accident of history which no longer has any force. It never held strictly for more than the peoples of western Europe and now that the Church is spread all over the world and the new nations of Asia and Africa are claiming their place, the need for a greater variety of rite and language, such as is forming in the Eastern churches, becomes even clearer.

On the other hand, one can overlook the fact that the Church comes before the bible and alone has the right to interpret it. One must also remember that christian worship is a sacrifice in the fullest and deepest sense, and this above all because of the very character of the biblical background from which it springs. Of course, there still remains much which is in dispute concerning the exact relation between scripture and tradition, the teaching authority of the Church and the nature of the sacraments, but these need no longer be matters of contention between warring camps, but subjects of discussion between those who share a common faith in Christ and a common desire for unity according to his will. The bible, accepted by all alike as the inspired word of God and interpreted according to what are now becoming accepted norms, provides a meeting ground for separated Christians as it has rarely done before.

Of course this does not mean that Catholics have to abandon the positions which have been acquired by theology in the course of history. But it does mean that scholastic theology has to recover its roots in the biblical tradition, which it possessed in the time of St Thomas. The theology of Aquinas was built on the foundations of a scriptural tradition, which he had inherited from the Fathers, and his *Summa* is a profound synthesis of this tradition with the new aristotelian philosophy. The modern theologian has to take account of the new positions which have been acquired by biblical and patristic study, while he remains firmly attached to the principles of Aquinas.

On the other hand, a Protestant will certainly expect a Catholic to show an acquaintance with the bible as deep and extensive as his own, and we may think that until he sees the bible taking the same place in the life of the ordinary Catholic as it does in his own, he will hardly be persuaded that the Catholic Church can offer him the fullness of life in Christ which he desires. In the same way, unless he finds in our Catholic churches a full participation of the laity in the liturgy and a full recognition of the place of the layman in the Church, he will still hesitate to recognize in the Catholic Church the true mystical body of Christ. Thus the present situation presents a challenge to the Catholic no less than to the Protestant, and it is only if both alike accept the challenge and are prepared to acknowledge the faults and imperfections of their conduct in the past, that we shall be able to hope for any real advance towards unity.

20. The Church Universal

IT IS OF particular importance for us at the present time to realize the universal character of the Church. Christianity has come to be regarded as the religion of the West and it is too often forgotten that it was an Asiatic religion before it was European, and that in the early days of the Church the principal sees were those of Antioch, Alexandria and Rome, representing Asia, Africa and Europe.

This vision of the universality of the Church is something which belongs not merely to the past but also to the future, and we need to keep it constantly before our minds. The Second Vatican Council raised great expectations that there would be a move towards the reunion of Christendom, especially in regard to the Eastern churches. But we must always remember that the great obstacle which keeps the Eastern churches from Rome is their fear of 'latinization'. The Latin Church has become so vast and so impressive in its organization that the lesser churches feel that they will be absorbed into it and lose their individuality.

It must be remembered that it is not merely a question of rites and ceremonies or even of language. The Eastern churches stand for a different tradition of Christianity, a different way of life and thought, which is yet essentially as orthodox and Catholic as the Latin. They have not only their own theology and spirituality, which are derived from the most ancient traditions of the Church. They look back to the great Greek Fathers and Doctors of the Church, Athanasius, John Chrysostom, Basil and Gregory and to the

Egyptian and Syrian Fathers who together with them laid
the foundations of the monastic life.

When we think of the expansion of the early Church we
tend to think of its extension to Greece and Rome and then
to France and Spain and the West. We sometimes forget that
its expansion to the East was no less impressive. We know
that Antioch was the first place where the 'disciples came to
be called Christians'; it is therefore in a special sense, after
Jerusalem, the mother of all the churches, and it was from
Antioch that the gospel was carried to the East. During the
first four centuries it spread all over Palestine, Syria, Mesopotamia and Persia and the number of its martyrs was equal
to that of the churches in the West. It was the first to witness
the birth of monasticism after Egypt, and the Syrian monks
rivalled, not only in numbers and austerity but also in holiness, their fellow monks in Egypt.

But what is of quite extraordinary interest is that this Syrian
Christianity was carried after this not only to India but also
right across Asia to China. In his book on the Mongol Mission, Christopher Dawson has shown that the Mongols of
central Asia were at one time very nearly converted to Christianity and that even the Chinese Emperor nearly became a
Christian. It is true that Syrian Christianity was by this time
affected by the nestorian heresy, but we are increasingly
recognizing that the separation of the Syrian and Egyptian
churches in the fifth century from Catholic unity was the
result not so much of heresy as of national feeling. It marks
the tragic turning point when the eastern peoples began to
separate from the West. The invasion of Islam came later in
the seventh century and gradually all these churches of Asia
and Africa were overwhelmed. At the present day only small
groups survive after centuries of islamic domination, the
majority still separated from Rome, but some of them reunited. If one stays in a city like Beirut today, one gets some

sense of the vitality and strength of these ancient churches. In Beirut one can find Syrian Catholics and Syrian Orthodox, Greek Catholics and Greek Orthodox, as well as Armenian and other rites, but the strongest Church is that of the Catholic Maronites, numbering over half a million, consisting of Syrian Christians who were reunited with Rome in the twelfth century.

It must be confessed that those churches which have been reunited with Rome, such as the Maronites in the Lebanon and the Syro-Malabar in South India, which numbers over a million, have suffered severely from latinization, and this forms one of the greatest obstacles to the reunion of the other Eastern churches. The case of the Syro-Malabar Church is, in fact, one of the great scandals of church history. When the Portuguese came to India in the sixteenth century they found a flourishing Syrian Church there. At first their relations with it were friendly, and they accepted it as Catholic. But when some nestorian formulas were found in the books of the Syrian Church (due to the influence, no doubt, of the Persian Church from which they received their orders), the Portuguese proceeded not only to eliminate these elements but to mutilate the whole rite so as to make it as like to the Latin rite as possible. The result of this disastrous action was to drive half the Church into a schism, which has yet to be healed. Happily, however, the Syro-Malabar rite is now being restored to its original form according to the instructions of the Holy See, and when the restoration is completed the Syro-Malabar Church will once again have its ancient liturgy.

This is but one example of a process, always at work, which tends to impose Latin rites and customs on the Eastern churches, which can only be overcome when Catholics as a whole come to recognize the true value of these Eastern rites and traditions. As I have said, it is not merely a matter of rites and ceremonies. The Eastern churches have their own languages, some of them like the Syriac and the Coptic (Egyptian) now 'dead' languages, but generally translated into the vernacular, in this case Arabic. This is itself one of the great advantages of the Eastern rites, that they have retained the custom of the ancient Church of using the vernacular in the liturgy, so that all the people are able to understand it and to take part in it. They also have their own gestures, characteristically eastern, which are very different from those of the Latin rite. In the Syrian rite, for instance, it is customary to stand with hands outstretched in prayer with palms upwards and to bow down in adoration by prostrating on both knees and touching the ground with the forehead. These are gestures which are found all over the Middle East, among Moslems no less than Christians, and constitute a typical eastern attitude of prayer.

With these different languages and gestures there go different forms of thought and expression. The Latin liturgy is peculiarly sober and restrained both in language and gestures, but the Eastern liturgies prefer a much more exuberant mode of expression. The Greek liturgy of St John Chrysostom, for instance, is full of the most profound symbolism and is one of the most beautiful expressions of christian piety in the world. But it is the Syrian liturgy which is distinguished above all for its poetry. It seems that while it was the Greek genius which gave to the Church its theology and the Latin genius its organization, it was the Syrian genius which gave it its poetry. The earliest christian poetry which we know, the Odes of Solomon, are believed to have come from Antioch in the second century, and both the *Gloria in Excelsis* and the beautiful evening hymn, 'Joyous Light', of the Greek Vespers, were originally Syrian compositions. But it was with St Ephrem in Mesopotamia in the fourth century that the Syrian genius found its true expression. St Ephrem composed hymns and songs to be sung by the people, so that it is said even women and children used to sing them in the street, and it was from this that the custom of singing hymns was introduced into the Church.

This has remained typical of the Syrian liturgy to the present day. Instead of psalms which take up so large a part of the Latin liturgy, the Syrian liturgy is composed of songs, that is original compositions, often of great beauty, in a regular rhythm put to music. These songs are mostly profound meditations on the scriptures, and this is what gives the Syrian liturgy its most important character. It is rooted in the bible and the biblical mode of thought. In other words it is entirely semitic in character. It is true that it owes its theology to the Greeks but it was the Syrian genius that translated this theology into poetry, so that the liturgy became a living expression of theology. It is this that gives the Syrian liturgy its great value at the present day. It gives us a true biblical theology. It is almost as though the Hebrew genius, which gave us the bible, had begun to flower again. The poetry springs from the same soil which gave us the poetry of the Old Testament and the Canticles of the New. It is in fact for the most part a deep meditation on the Old Testament in the light of the New, and on the New Testament in the light of a developed theology.

In other words we have in the Syrian Church, as in all the Eastern churches to some extent, a theology which has not lost its roots in the bible and the liturgy. It has been our misfortune in the West that theology and liturgy have grown apart, so that theology has become a science separated from prayer and prayer has in turn become separated from theology and grown sentimental. But in the Eastern Church, liturgy has always remained the great school of theology and theology has never lost its contact with the biblical mode of thought. Instead of being an abstract rational system, as it has become in the West, it has retained a mystical and symbolic character, which makes it a school of contemplation

not of abstract thought. No doubt to have developed a
rational and scientific system of theology, as scholasticism
has done, is something of permanent value and a necessary
stage in the development of the Church. But theologians
today are feeling the need to return to the sources of theology, to the bible and the liturgy, and to recover that unity
of theology, liturgy and spirituality which was characteristic of the early Church.

It is here that the Eastern churches have so much to give.
The reconciliation of the Eastern churches would be the
means of the recovery of precious elements in the christian
tradition, which have been obscured, though never actually
lost, in the development of the Church in the West. It would
mean the recovery of the biblical tradition of theology, of a
theology which keeps near to the symbolical thought of
the bible and never loses its mystical character; it would
mean the recovery of a liturgical tradition which acts as a
living source of theology and enables the people by its symbolism to participate in the deepest experience of the Church's
life, in the fullness of the mystery of Christ; and finally it
would mean the recovery of the full sense of the Church as
the mystical body of Christ, each Church and each congrega-
tion representing the body of Christ and all united in an
organic whole, witnessing to the mystery of the presence of
Christ on earth. These are the goals which are being sought
by the biblical movement, the liturgical movement and the
development of the doctrine of the mystical body of Christ
in the West, but it is only with the union of the Eastern
churches that we can hope for their full realization.

In this way one might hope that the Church would recover her full catholicity, uniting both East and West in a
unity which transcends both time and space. She would
appear then no longer as a western European organization,
but as belonging equally to Europe, Asia and Africa (and of
course to America and Australia). At present the Latin lit-

urgy has been spread all over the world, but this extension of a uniform rite in the East and West is not according to the original genius of the Church. In the early Church, rites and languages were always adapted to the different peoples to whom the gospel was preached. One may hope that when the Latin rite is translated everywhere into the vernacular and is able to adapt its external customs, its music and vestments and ceremonial, to the requirements of the different cultures in which it is found, it may become a true expression of the religious life of these different peoples.

But it would seem clear that the Eastern liturgies have also a very important part to play in this development. The Syrian rite seems to be particularly adapted to Asia, not only to the Middle East where it has long been established but also to the Far East, where it once penetrated so deeply and where it still survives in South India. It would seem also that the Egyptian rite (which is said in Arabic), and still more the Ethiopian rite, have a very important place in the African Church. The Ethiopian rite, I have been told, is a distinctive African development of the ancient Coptic rite and, by the use of music, drums and dances, as well as a distinctive church architecture derived from native tradition, is wonderfully adapted to the African genius.

But still more important than the external forms of the liturgy (though these are of incalculable importance) is the inner spirit of the Eastern rites. In them we find the true genius of the christian East. By their symbolic and mystical character they will make an appeal to the eastern mind which the more sober Latin rite can never have. We are now living at a moment in history when East and West are coming into contact as they have never done before. The people of Asia and Africa are awaking to a new life, in which they are becoming conscious of the deep values of their own cultural inheritance, while they are adapting themselves to the customs of the West. It is essential that the Church should be presented to these people as the embodiment of the genius both of East and West, as an institution which belongs equally to East and West, adapting herself to every human culture because of her inmost essence she transcends all and has it in her power to break down the 'wall of partition' between East and West and to reconcile all men in one body in Christ.

It would be foolish to expect an ecumenical council to achieve all this, but we can hope and pray that it may lead to a better understanding with the Eastern churches. Above all we can try to cultivate in ourselves a truly catholic spirit, seeing beyond the boundaries of the Latin Church and the civilization which has grown up under its influence in the West, so that we can include the great cultures of India, China and Japan in our vision, together with the islamic world and those primitive but profound cultures which have shaped the African mind. We should be able to see all these cultures as so many fields in which the gospel has still to be preached and where the Church can grow to her full stature as the bride of Christ.

21. The Church of the Future

WHEN Pope John first summoned the Vatican Council he put before it three objectives. The first was the renewal of the Catholic Church from within; the second was the reunion of Christendom through the development of an ecumenical spirit in relation to the separated churches; the third was the manifestation of the mission of the Church to the world.

These three objectives cannot, of course, be taken altogether separately; each is implied in the other. The renewal of the Church has been shown to be intimately related to the ecumenical attitude towards separated Christians, and the mission of the Church to the world is in turn largely dependent on the development of a renewed and reunited Christianity. Yet we can see that there is a difference of emphasis and the emphasis of the first sessions of the council was clearly on the interior renewal of the Church.

The adoption of the schema on the liturgy, especially that part of it which concerns the use of the vernacular, has opened the way to a renewal of the christian spirit, which has been sought ever since Pius X published his encyclical on the liturgy, in which he said that the full participation of the laity in the liturgy of the Church was the indispensable source of the christian spirit. But it is only now that the reforms have been made which make this participation possible. As long as the language and a great many of the ceremonies of the liturgy are unintelligible to the majority of Christians it is idle to expect any serious renewal of the christian spirit. But now that the principles of a complete renewal of the liturgy have been drafted and approved, there is nothing which stands in the way, unless it should be the failure on the part of the different hierarchies to put these principles into practice.

The debate on the place of the bishop in the Church in relation to the pope, which occupied so much time in the second session of the council, is also an important element in the renewal of the Church. Nothing stands so much in the way of creating an image of the Church as truly catholic and universal as the impression which is given of the Church as a vast monolith with the pope at its head and the bishops occupying a position of inferiority, totally subordinate to him. This was, of course, never wholly true, but it cannot be denied that the place of the bishop in the Church has not been fully realized since the Council of Trent, or even since Hildebrand. It may be said that already one of the principal effects of the Vatican Council in having brought so many bishops to Rome is that it has awakened this consciousness among the bishops, and however the place of the bishop may eventually be defined, it is impossible that this consciousness should be lost.

It need hardly be said how much this will affect the attitude of the Eastern churches to the Catholic Church. The one really serious obstacle to the reunion of East and West is the position of the pope. The Orthodox feel with some justice that the papacy had undergone a long evolution in the West, which has taken it very far in many respects from the position which it occupied in the early centuries. But once the principle of the collegiality of the bishops as successors of the apostles is finally established and the supreme authority of the Church is seen to reside alike in the bishops with the pope at their head and in the pope as the head of the college of bishops, but in neither apart from the other, then the possibility of the acceptance of such a position by the Orthodox churches becomes very real.

In any case, the acceptance of the principle of diversity in the Church, not only in liturgy, but also in theology, in spirituality and in discipline, which was brought out so strongly in the council, opens the way to breaking down the image of a monolithic unity and to giving the Eastern churches the position which belongs to them by right. As long as the idea remains that the Latin Church, with its liturgy and theology and canon law, is the norm for the whole Catholic Church there can be no hope of any serious rapprochment with the East. We have to realize that the traditions of the Eastern churches are just as ancient and venerable as those of the Roman Church and that for the most part they are quite independent of it. Greek and Russian theology and spirituality, its customs of a married clergy and the use of icons, and so many other diversities, which belong to the Eastern churches, set them apart from the Latin church, not in any position of inferiority but as sister churches, expressing differences of culture which are absolutely necessary if the Church is to realise her true catholicity.

Thus the renewal of the Church from within has already begun to open the way to the reunion of Christendom, at least in regard to the great world of Orthodoxy. But this conception of cultural differences in the Church has also a definite bearing on the third objective of the council, the mission of the Church to the world. The problems of the Church in the face of the modern world in regard to poverty, race, war and such matters of burning importance came up for discussion in the fourth session under the famous 'Schema 13'.

But the question of the relation of the Church to other religions is perhaps the most fundamental problem of all, because it concerns the very nature of the Church and divine revelation. The Church is confronted today with at least three other religions, Hinduism, Buddhism and Islam, each claiming to be universal and each numbering several hundred million followers. So far the attitude of the Church to such religions has been mainly negative. They have been regarded as 'false' religions and no attempt has been made to come to terms with them. But it is clear now, as a result of the council, that such an attitude cannot be maintained. It is a hopeful sign that the present pope should have established the Secretariat for non-Christian Religions, whose work runs parallel with that for Christian Unity. Now that this has come into existence, the whole problem of the relation of the Church to these other religions, that is of the mission of the Church in the strict sense, will have to be faced.

It seems clear that what is required is an extension of the principle of the ecumenical movement among Christians to the sphere of our relations with other religions. It is not possible in the modern world to go out to 'convert' Muslims, Buddhists or Hindus. Such an attitude only produces resentment and often a violent reaction. We have to learn to approach the Muslim, the Buddhist and the Hindu as we have learned to approach our separated brethren among Christians. We have first of all to learn to meet them with love and respect, recognizing that each one is our brother, sons of a common Father and called like us to eternal life. It is only on this basis that any real encounter between the Church and other religions can take place.

We have then to learn to understand these other religions and to see them in their true relation to the Church. This may involve a certain development in our theology, but the principles of such a development seem to be clear. It cannot be doubted that the way of salvation is open to all men. Christ assumed the nature of all men, died for all men and redeemed all mankind. There is therefore no man from the first to the last man who is outside this saving economy of grace. When we ask ourselves how this saving grace of Christ reaches those who are outside the visible sphere of the

Church, the principles of an answer are given by tradition. Aquinas himself, asking the question how men could be saved before the coming of Christ, replies that though they could not have an explicit faith in Christ, they could have an implicit faith, in as much as they had faith in divine providence, since 'belief in his providence includes all those things which God dispenses in time for man's salvation' (S.T., iia, iiae, i, 7).

There is therefore the possibility of an implicit faith in Christ, through which a man can be saved, wherever there is a genuine faith in divine providence. This is what is sometimes called the Covenant of the Natural Law, or the Cosmic Covenant. It extends to all men without exception and it is to this 'cosmic' covenant that such religions as Hinduism, Buddhism and Islam belong, though in Islam we have to recognize also positive influences from both Judaism and Christianity. Thus we cannot look upon the Hindu, the Buddhist or the Muslim as outside the covenant of grace. Through the elements of truth in their religion, which derive from this cosmic revelation, by which God makes himself known through nature and conscience, they belong to the economy of grace. There is already a 'presence' of Christ and therefore of the Church in all genuine religion, however hidden it may be.

It is our task, therefore, to meet this presence of Christ in our brothers in other religions, as we have learned to meet it in our separated christian brothers. Just as we recognize a common faith and baptism and a common bible with other Christians, we have to recognize an implicit faith and desire for baptism (in so far as they believe in and desire God's will for their salvation) and the elements of a common revelation in every religion. It is obvious that this involves a considerable rethinking of our conception of the mission of the Church. We have to acknowledge that the Church has not only to teach but also to learn from other religions. We have

to seek for those elements of truth which exist in each
religion and try to present the gospel not simply in opposition to such religion but as its fulfilment.

The reform of the liturgy already suggests the way in which
the Church could divest herself of western forms in the
liturgy by adopting the language and soon one may hope the
music and art and architecture of the different peoples of the
world, instead of clinging to the outmoded forms of Gothic
and Baroque. But a more serious problem arises in regard
to theology. Must we continue to present our Catholic doctrine in terms borrowed from Greek philosophy? It is now
coming to be recognized that just as unity in sacramental
worship can be expressed in diverse forms of liturgy, so
unity in faith can find expression in various forms of theology. We have already a Greek and a Latin theology which
differ not only in their expression but also in their mode of
thought. Can we not conceive a theology which would make
use of the modes of thought and expression of the Vedanta
or of Confucian philosophy, just as the Fathers and Aquinas
made use of Greek philosophy?

Such a diversity both in liturgy and theology would be in
harmony with the new understanding of the government of
the Church which is coming into light as a result of the
Vatican Council. The movement now is towards a decentral-
ization of the Church, which would allow much greater
freedom for the bishops' conferences in the different parts
of the world. In this way one could envisage a return to
something like the old patriarchal system, by which the
great patriarchates, Antioch, Alexandria, Constantinople and
Rome each constituted a separate 'province' of the Church
with its own distinct liturgy and school of theology and
system of Church government.

It is not difficult to conceive on these lines how we might
eventually see new churches rising in India, China and Japan
and in different parts of Africa, each having its own distinc-

tive cultural forms, adapted to the traditions of the different people, with its own liturgy, its own forms of theology and its own system of church government. At the same time the speed of communication today makes it easy for all churches to keep in touch with the centre, so that the unity of the Church, with its one faith and sacramental order and its hierarchy acknowledging the pope as the successor of St Peter and the head of the whole Church, would not be endangered.

Such a development would open the way to a genuine ecumenical spirit towards the different religions of the world, by which the Church would be able to meet each of them at the deepest level of its doctrine and spiritual life. On the part of the Church there would be a profound assimilation of the cultural forms of these religions, particularly their philosophy and their spiritual discipline. On the part of the other religions there would be the possibility of a real confrontation with the mystery of Christ, not presented under alien cultural forms but in a manner which would bring out the deep affinities existing in all the great religious traditions. In this meeting every kind of syncretism, of course, has to be avoided, which might impoverish the truth of the christian message. But this is exactly what the Greek and Latin Fathers accomplished in regard to Greek philosophy and Roman Law. To undertake this synthesis with the Vedanta, and Mahayana Buddhism, with Chinese and islamic philosophy is surely the task of the Church of the future.

Acknowledgments

Grateful thanks to the following journals for permission to reprint copyright material: *Commonweal, New Blackfriars, Search, Good Work, Pax, Jubilee, One in Christ, Clergy Monthly* and the *Pax Romana Journal.*